DATA
RULES

ALSO BY JIM KNIGHT

The Definitive Guide to Instructional Coaching:
Seven Factors for Success

Evaluating Instructional Coaching:
People, Programs, and Partnership

The Instructional Playbook:
The Missing Link for Translating Research into Practice

DATA

JIM KNIGHT
MICHAEL FAGGELLA-LUBY

RULES

ELEVATING TEACHING
WITH OBJECTIVE
REFLECTION

ONE FINE BIRD  PRESS / LAWRENCE, KANSAS

ascd
Arlington, Virginia USA

2800 Shirlington Road, Suite 1001 • Arlington, VA 22206 USA

Phone: 800-933-2723 or 703-578-9600

Website: www.ascd.org • Email: member@ascd.org

Author guidelines: www.ascd.org/write

Richard Culatta, *Executive Director*; Anthony Rebora, *Chief Content Officer*; Genny Ostertag, *Managing Director, Book Acquisitions & Editing*; Susan Hills, *Senior Acquisitions Editor*; Mary Beth Nielsen, *Director, Book Editing*; Megan Doyle, *Editor*; Georgia Park, *Senior Graphic Designer*; Valerie Younkin, *Senior Production Designer*; Kelly Marshall, *Production Manager*; Shajuan Martin, *E-Publishing Specialist*; Christopher Logan, *Senior Production Specialist*; Kathryn Oliver, *Creative Project Manager*

ONE FINE BIRD/PRESS

853 N. 1663 Road

Lawrence, KS 66049

Phone: 308-496-4724 • E-mail: hello@instructionalcoaching.com

Website: www.instructionalcoaching.com

Edited by Kirsten McBride

Cover Design by Chase Christensen

Interior Design by Chase Christensen

All web links in this book are correct as of the publication date below but may have become inactive or otherwise modified since that time. If you notice a deactivated or changed link, please email books@ascd.org with the words "Link Update" in the subject line. In your message, please specify the web link, the book title, and the page number on which the link appears.

PAPERBACK ISBN: 978-1-4166-3330-3   ASCD product #123026   n9/24

PDF E-BOOK ISBN: 978-1-4166-3331-0; see Books in Print for other formats.

Quantity discounts are available: email programteam@ascd.org or call 800-933-2723, ext. 5773, or 703-575-5773. For desk copies, go to www.ascd.org/deskcopy.

Library of Congress Cataloging-in-Publication Data

Names: Knight, Jim, author. | Faggella-Luby, Michael, author.

Title: Data rules : elevating teaching with objective reflection / Jim Knight, Michael Faggella-Luby.

Description: Arlington, VA : ASCD, 2024. | Includes bibliographical references and index.

Identifiers: LCCN 2024026333 (print) | LCCN 2024026334 (ebook) | ISBN 9781416633303 (paperback) | ISBN 9781416633310 (adobe pdf) | ISBN 9781416633327 (epub)

Subjects: LCSH: Educational evaluation--Data processing. | Educational leadership--Data processing. | Educational indicators.

Classification: LCC LB2822.75 .K655 2024 (print) | LCC LB2822.75 (ebook) | DDC 370.72--dc23/eng/20240718

LC record available at https://lccn.loc.gov/2024026333

LC ebook record available at https://lccn.loc.gov/2024026334

33 32 31 30 29 28 27 26 25 24   1 2 3 4 5 6 7 8 9 10 11 12

TABLE OF CONTENTS

//.

DEDICATED TO

This book is dedicated to Dr. Don Deshler, our advisor, mentor, and friend. Don's guidance has meant the world to us. We would not have written this book if we had not had the great good fortune to work with Don.

PREFACE

We admit it. Data generally don't make for the most exciting topic of conversation. When people ask us what book we're working on and we mention data, most of the time only the nerdiest of the nerds seem to respond with excitement, while others quickly move on to other topics or turn away to other conversation partners. Then again, maybe you are like some of our friends who think differently about data. If not, we hope this book will change your mind.

To us, data are important, fascinating, and at the heart of meaningful change. If we want to get better at almost anything, we need data. Whether we want to qualify for the Boston Marathon, lose 10 pounds, save up for a home, or empower our students, data are essential. Data help us see where we are, where we want to go, and how much progress we're making on our journey to our goal.

Used effectively, data can be motivating, illuminating, and incredibly helpful. Used ineffectively, data can suck the life out of us, decreasing morale, knocking down the esteem of everyone on the receiving end. In short, data are powerful and essential but must be used appropriately.

While doing some of the original research on instructional coaching with school districts in Kansas, Jim and his team realized that they needed more clarity around how to provide support to create learner-friendly classrooms, set goals, and measure improvements in classroom culture. Jim reached out to Randy Sprick, the founder of Safe and Civil Schools and one of the originators of positive behavior supports, and Wendy Reinke, now a researcher at the University of Missouri. Randy and Wendy became partners in the research, eventually co-authoring with us a book on classroom management. Those early collaborations around data eventually led Jim to Michael and what eventually became this book.

Our growing understanding of data soon led us to the conclusion that every successful change leader—whether a coach, administrator, or leader—needs to understand why gathering data is important and how to gather data. There are at least four reasons why data gathering is an essential part of growth and change.

First, when people understand data, they are able to see what they otherwise might not see. Teachers who watch videos of their lessons and gather data on students' responses to questions, for example, may realize that some groups of students are not participating in learning opportunities afforded to them in the classroom. And such insight can prompt teachers to make changes that lead to more equitable and effective learning for all students.

Second, when people understand data, they are able to talk with more precision about how students engage and learn and how teachers teach. For example, when a teacher and coach understand educational author Julie Stern's distinction between acquiring, connecting, or transferring knowledge, they can more accurately talk about the kind of learning or assessment that is needed in a class. A richer, shared vocabulary leads to better conversations, and that is especially important when it comes to data.

Third, data help people identify goals. Our research has shown that setting student-focused goals and assessing engagement or achievement are vitally important. And to set an engagement or achievement goal, you need to know what you're going to measure. For example, a better understanding of emotional engagement can help us set a goal that effectively measures whether or not students feel hope and, therefore, are more likely to succeed in school. That kind of clarity is essential because, as our friend coaching expert John Campbell has said many times, "if there is no goal, it's just a nice conversation."

Lastly, data help build confidence and agency in both students and teachers. When students see progress, their interest in learning grows, and just like children playing video games, they can get hooked on positive feedback. Teresa Amabile and Steven Kramer (2011) have labeled this phenomenon "the progress principle." Progress is also important for teachers. When teachers see measurable improvements in student engagement or learning, they recognize that their actions make a difference and, as a result, they become more motivated and more committed to coaching or other efforts to improve outcomes in the classroom.

Data, then, constitute an essential part of improvement. Data help us see what we might not see, give us words to talk with precision about learning and achievement, help us set goals, and build student and teacher confidence as everyone strives to meet those goals. In short, if you want to see improvement in schools, you need to understand data. That is why we created this book. Whether you are a teacher, an administrator, or a coach, we hope *Data Rules* will help you do this incredibly important, complex work of increasing student learning, engagement, and well-being. We also hope the book will help you see clearly what a powerful, positive impact you are having on children.

ACKNOWLEDGMENTS

FROM MICHAEL FAGGELLA-LUBY

As a first-time author, I could not have asked for a more generous mentor and collaborator than Jim. Our conversations have sharpened my thinking and provided deep insights into our shared care for and sense of responsibility to educators reading this work, always leaving me ready for more. Thank you, Jim, for your wisdom, kindness, and willingness to forgive that I am a fan of the Boston Bruins.

A book project of this scope has only been possible thanks to the incredible personal and professional communities I am fortunate enough to inhabit. While I am grateful to each member of these communities who have provided advice, encouragement, and wisdom throughout the process, there are a few I feel compelled to mention specifically. First, I want to thank my co-advisor, Dr. Jean Schumaker, who instilled in me a love of research in service of improving outcomes for students, particularly students who struggle to learn. Her tireless efforts to improve my writing are hopefully reflected in this book.

Second, I want to thank my colleagues at Texas Christian University, particularly those affiliated with the Alice Neeley Special Education Research & Service (ANSERS) Institute. You provide a safe, supportive, and insightful sounding board that has allowed ideas in this collaboration to germinate and grow. I enjoy working with each of you and am grateful for your many gifts. I also want to thank the small army of graduate students who helped support my research on different iterations of this project over the years. I hope that our collaborations enhanced your analytical skills, made you curious, and inspired you as future educators and leaders in our field.

Finally, I want to thank my family. While I am part of many communities, there is only one home. I am lucky to live near my in-laws, Dan and Theresa, whose boundless generosity of time and talent is an inspiration to me every day. When people ask me where I am from, I love to quote John Adams in claiming that "Massachusetts is my country," and I have my wonderful parents, Dan and Sally, back there to thank for the gifts of life, a love of learning, and a willingness to work hard. I miss you every day, so thank goodness for FaceTime!

My love of education and passion for improving outcomes for children began a long time ago teaching at Bishop Kenny High School in Jacksonville, Florida, but no love, passion, or learning can parallel the joy of being the father of Jack and Claire. I know it seems like I am always working—except when I am playing Legos, helping you run lines for a play, or chauffeuring you around – but I am really just constantly marveling at the wonder of you both. You inspire me every day to try to make the world a better place for you to live in. Finally, if you are lucky enough to marry your best friend, then you know the unshakable love and joy that make home, well ... home. My wife, Kate, is the best partner, co-parent, and source of *agape* I could have ever asked for in this life—and I have 25 years of data to prove it!

FROM JIM KNIGHT

I'm not 100 percent certain that this is true, but my guess is that if you look up "patience" in the dictionary, you will find a picture of my co-author, Michael Faggella-Luby. Michael has shown amazing patience and a great sense of humor during the collaboration on this project. I'm sure there were moments when he wondered if this book would ever be completed, and no doubt there have been times when he was tempted to quit. But I'm so glad that he stuck with me through it all, because his contribution has been invaluable. While Michael might have written this book without me, I could not have written it without him. Most important to me, Michael's caring for others, especially children, has helped me find a new friend.

Anything I write at this point is really part of a team effort, and I am especially grateful to my colleagues at the Instructional Coaching Group (ICG). Together we are building a different kind of company, an organization where making a difference in the lives of children is the driving force behind all we do. I'm grateful for your ideas, creativity, hard work, and especially for your commitment to our goal of excellent instruction, every day, in every class, for every student, everywhere.

Along with my colleagues at ICG, I'm also grateful to my colleagues in Australia at Growth Coaching International (GCI), in particular my two good friends, John Campbell and Christian van Nieuwerburgh. Additionally, I'm deeply indebted to the hundreds of coaches from around the world who have taught me about what works and doesn't work when it comes to coaching, learning, and especially how data informs learning and growth.

I've also been extremely fortunate to work with two outstanding editors. Susan Hills at ASCD helped Michael and me shape this book into what we hope will be a very helpful tool for many educators. Susan, I'm grateful for your ideas, wisdom, and especially for your enthusiasm and support. Kirsten McBride has edited every book I've written since 2006, and her record still stands. I have yet to write one page that Kirsten couldn't improve. If my writing is clear and effective, there is a good chance Kirsten has helped me make it that. I feel so much more confidence as a writer knowing that Kirsten will help me be better.

This book, like many other publications at ICG, was designed by Chase Christensen. Chase's good taste, commitment to beauty, and gifted design have greatly contributed to our company. I am deeply grateful to Chase for his work on this book and many other projects at ICG over the years.

Most important, I'm grateful to my family. My children—Geoff, Cameron, David, Emily, Ben, Isaiah, and Luke—you are my inspiration. I'm grateful and proud of all you do to make the world a better place. And my wife, Jenny, you are without doubt the greatest contributor to any positive impact I've had. In fact, it's no coincidence that almost everything I've created came after I met you. Your belief in me has made all the difference, and I'm profoundly grateful for all the support you've shown me over the years.

ONE FINE BIRD PRESS GRATEFULLY ACKNOWLEDGES THE CONTRIBUTIONS OF THE FOLLOWING REVIEWERS:

Lindsey Bingley
Literacy and Numeracy
Strategist
Calgary, AB, Canada

Kamina Fitzgerald EdD
District Academic Coach &
Beginning Teacher Mentor
North Carolina

Deacon Godsey
Researcher,
Instructional Coaching Group
Lawrence, Kansas

Amy Musante
Consultant,
Instructional Coaching Group
Lawrence, Kansas

Krista Scott, EdD
Director of Teacher
Development,
Andrews Independent
School District

Morris G White, MS
Math Specialist and Educator
Western United States

Chase Christensen
Director of Design,
Instructional Coaching Group
Lawrence, Kansas

Michelle Harris
Director of Consulting,
Instructional Coaching Group
Lawrence, Kansas

Heather Macchi
Math Specialist,
Wellesley Public Schools
Wellesley, Massachusetts

Bobbie Noall, PhD
Lead Program Facilitator of
the GRREC ED KY Rank Change
Program and Literacy Consultant
for GRREC
Bowling Green, Kentucky

Sharon Thomas
Director of K-12 and Family
Engagement Programs,
Touchstones Discussion Project
Stevensville, Maryland

Kristin Crouch
Instructional Coach,
Rensselaer City School District
Rensselaer, New York

David Higginson
International Educator
and Tech Coach
Cambodia

Nasreen McDowell
Manager of Partnerships
and Outreach,
Instructional Coaching Group
Lawrence, Kansas

Ruth Ryschon
Copyeditor,
Instructional Coaching Group
Lawrence, Kansas

Mark Verde
Assistant Principal,
Bangkok Patana School
Bangkok, Thailand

THE HERO IS THE DATA

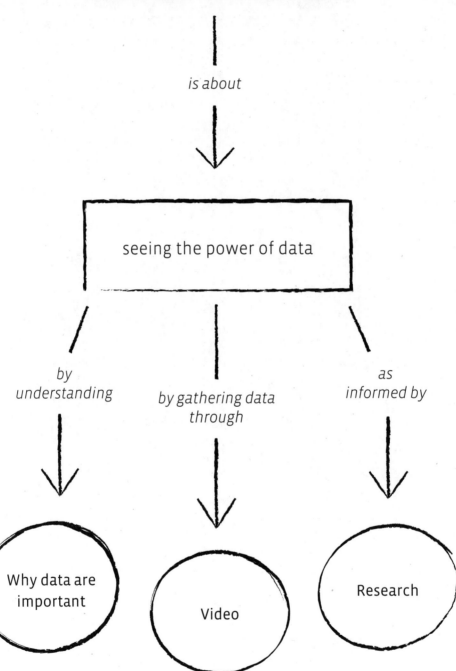

is about

seeing the power of data

by understanding

by gathering data through

as informed by

Why data are important

Video

Research

CHAPTER 1

THE HERO IS THE DATA

This chapter presents an outline of the many reasons why gathering data is important, guidelines for introducing and using video in a school district to gather data, and an overview of the research related to the kinds of data we've included in the book. You can skip it if you want to dive right into the book, but maybe consider reading the opening story to see if this is a chapter you want to spend some time with.

CHAPTER 1 RESOURCES

Access charts, diagrams, research, and resources from this chapter.

Using stats the way that we read them, we'll find the value in players that nobody else can see.

PETER BRAND

The movie *Moneyball*, based on Michael Lewis's nonfiction book with the same name, tells the story of Billy Beane, the Oakland Athletics general manager. In 2002, Beane turned the undermanned Athletics into a competitive baseball team by acting on the unconventional advice he received from Peter Brand, a young Yale economics graduate. Faced with having to replace several high-profile players, Beane followed Brand's suggestion to sign players based on a different understanding of what it takes to win in baseball. The Athletics didn't win the World Series that year, but they did have a very successful year, setting a new Major League record for winning the most games in a row in a season. At the end of the movie, Beane turns down an offer from the Boston Red Sox to become the highest-paid general manager in sports history. Two years later Boston, using Beane's methods, won the World Series for the first time since 1918. The game of baseball hasn't been the same since.

Beane is the central character and the person we root for when we watch the movie, but he's not the hero; in fact, the movie's hero isn't a person. The hero is the data.

Billy Beane made the Athletics a competitive team and ultimately revolutionized baseball by using data to get better. Acting on the innovative insights of sabermetrician Bill James, Brand used data to see what other teams couldn't see—that on-base percentage (how often players get on base) is more important than batting average (how often players get hits). Gathering and analyzing data helped Brand and later Beane recognize that the flashy number, batting average, helped players get big salaries, but it was the more workman-like number, on-base percentage, that won games.

Data, as Brand says in the movie, helped the Athletics "find the value in players that nobody else can see." And as a result, the Athletics got better and won.

Data's reach goes far beyond sports. Temperature tells us what we should wear each day. The Dow Jones tells us whether we should look for a second job, and our weight, blood pressure, and body mass index tell us whether we should use the money from our second job to buy a book about plant-based diets. Used correctly, data can help us see where we are, where we want to be, and what we need to do to hit our goals. Used incorrectly, data can keep us from seeing what is most important all around us. In baseball, the general managers who focused on batting average missed seeing the importance of on-base percentage. In schools, leaders who obsessively focus on achievement scores can miss other important data, such as students' engagement and well-being. But more important, data can help us see people that we might not otherwise see, as was the case with Billy Beane.

Why Data Are Essential

Like sports, schools are rich in data, and schools may or may not use data effectively. In our studies of coaching at the Instructional Coaching Group in Lawrence, Kansas, and the Kansas Coaching Project at the University of Kansas Center for Research on Learning, we have found that data are essential for all improvement efforts in schools, whether we are talking about teachers coaching themselves, teachers coaching each other, teachers working with coaches, teams or professional learning communities engaged in collaborative inquiry, schools undertaking schoolwide improvement initiatives, or teachers having evaluation conversations with administrators. When people are trying to get better at what they do, they use data to guide the process.

Data are essential in schools for many reasons. First, data help professional learners get a clear picture of reality. Most professionals do not really know what it looks like when they do what they do (Knight, 2014). This is true of coaches, teachers, and principals; in fact, pretty much anyone who watches themselves on video. Ho and Kane

(2013) underscored this challenge in their attempts to understand reliability and accuracy across thousands of hours of observation by teachers and administrators as part of the two-year Measures of Effective Teaching (MET) project funded by the Bill and Melinda Gates Foundation (2009).

The simple truth is that our views of reality are shaped significantly by perceptual errors and defense mechanisms that lead us to make poorly informed decisions about our work and our lives.

COMMON PERCEPTUAL ERRORS

(based on definitions from *The Definitive Guide to Instructional Coaching* [Knight, 2022])

CONFIRMATION BIAS: The tendency to consciously or unconsciously seek out data that reinforce our assumptions.

ATTRIBUTION ERROR: The habit of blaming others for our missteps but excusing ourselves for the same mistakes.

STEREOTYPING: Overgeneralizing the characteristics of people in a group.

PRIMACY EFFECT: Our bias toward overgeneralizing our first experiences with a person or information source.

HALO EFFECT: The tendency to assume that a person has many positive characteristics after seeing them exhibit just one positive characteristic.

HABITUATION: The tendency to stop noticing the unique features of something we experience all the time.

COMMON DEFENSE MECHANISMS

(based on definitions from *The Definitive Guide to Instructional Coaching* [Knight, 2022])

DENIAL AND MINIMIZATION: Choosing not to see unpleasant data.

RATIONALIZATION: Justifying our behavior even if our justifications are irrational.

BLAMING OTHERS: Excusing our situation by blaming or scapegoating others.

BLAMING OURSELVES: Failing to acknowledge reality by blaming ourselves for unpleasant occurrences.

An imperfect view of reality isn't entirely a bad thing. As Shankar Vedantam and Bill Mesler explain in *Useful Delusions* (2021), life can be so difficult and challenging that some misperceptions of reality can be helpful; in fact, they may be essential in parenting, facing illness, or how you address a pandemic. Seeing reality in its brutal harshness all the time might be too difficult for anyone. But, if we want to learn and grow, we need to see reality clearly.

In education, data help educators see, understand, and describe what is happening in their classrooms more effectively. A clear understanding of the reality surfaced by data—such as how engaged students are, the percentage of instructional time focused on learning, the number of times teachers focus positive attention on their students, and so forth—is often a catalyst for change, prompting professionals to seek out ways to improve. Educators who use data to better understand what is happening in their classrooms often feel driven to change, motivated by a desire to see more of something they like (e.g., student engagement) or less of something they don't like (e.g., wasted time). These educators have a way of getting what they want out of their students and themselves.

Data also help educators identify where they need to focus their improvement efforts to have the most positive impact on children's lives. When people interested in change don't have the clear picture of reality provided by data, they risk focusing a lot of effort on changes that will have little impact on children's lives. For example, a teacher who tries to engage students by using extrinsic motivation such as rewards may find from data that, while rewards might have a quick, short-lived impact, they won't address the more fundamental issues—relevance—and that, instead, the true high-leverage area for improvement lies in creating assignments that students can apply to their lives.

Finally, data have a very practical importance in that they provide educators a way to identify a finish line and measure progress toward that finish line. In our work with schools and coaches, we have learned that goals are an essential part of any improvement process, even within a continuous improvement cycle marked by iterative and incremental improvements. In fact, one of the most important questions we can ask ourselves or our collaborating educators as we start out on a change initiative is "If the goal is hit, what will be different or better for my students?"

Seeing the Data

Apple's invention and mass adoption of the iPhone revolutionized how data are gathered in classrooms by giving almost every teacher an easy way to record video of their lessons. More recently, since the COVID-19 pandemic forced everyone to work from home, digital communication platforms like Zoom, Teams, and Skype have made video a more regular part of the educator landscape.

Before the ease of the iPhone in our pockets, data were gathered by observers, such as principals, and shared with teachers afterward since video was too cumbersome to use. Such conversations often fail for two reasons. First, many teachers do not have a clear picture of how students are experiencing their classroom and, therefore, do not agree with what they are told by observers and naturally assume that the principal's observations are wrong.

Second, observers often gather data unreliably. Principals may have too little training in how to gather data, have too little knowledge to know what to look for, and may let too much time pass between when they observe a class and fill in the report. Finally, teachers are often frustrated when one administrator observes their classroom and says one thing, and another administrator observes the class and says something else.

Using video resolves all these issues. First, video provides teachers with a clear picture of reality so that they can clearly see what is happening in the classroom.

Second, observers can make sure that their observations are correct by reviewing sections of a recording of a lesson multiple times, as needed.

Despite these advantages, one drawback to video is that few people like to see recordings of themselves. There aren't many people who watch videos of themselves and say, "Wow, I'm younger and thinner than I thought." For this reason, it is important for educational leaders to create psychologically safe environments to encourage teachers to use video. Jim identifies six guidelines for increasing the likelihood that video will be embraced in a school (Knight, 2014).

Establish Trust

We have found that openness to using video varies more by school than it does by person. In many schools, most teachers feel comfortable using video to coach themselves, with coaches, with teams, and as a part of their evaluation. In other schools, few if any teachers are willing to use video. The most likely reason for this discrepancy is trust. When teachers feel they can trust their administrators and their peers, they say yes to video. When educators don't feel trust, they shy away from the vulnerable experience of watching recordings of themselves.

Trust, as Jim has written (Knight, 2015), involves at least five factors:

1. **CHARACTER:** We trust people we see acting in ethical ways; people who are honest and transparent.

2. **RELIABILITY:** We trust people who do what they say they are going to do when they say they are going to do it.

3. **COMPETENCE:** We trust people who have a deep understanding of what they describe; effective instruction.

4. **WARMTH:** We are more inclined to trust people who are good listeners and are kind, positive, attentive, and validating.

5. **STEWARDSHIP:** We trust people who have our best interests at heart.

Give Choices

Leaders may be tempted to tell all their teachers that they must use video as a part of their professional development and personal evaluation. No matter how well intentioned such a request is, telling people what to do, especially professionals, is rarely a good strategy for change, and that is especially true for something as emotionally complex as watching yourself on video.

Use Intrinsic Motivation

People are more likely to embrace video when they see it as a power tool to help them get better. As Harvard researcher Theresa Amabile concluded after reviewing thousands of data points from interviews, observations, and surveys of teams in action, "Managers who say—or secretly believe—that employees work better under pressure, uncertainty, unhappiness, or fear are just plain wrong" (Amabile & Kramer, 2011, p. 58).

Establish Boundaries

Some teachers hesitate to use video because they do not know how video will be used. Leaders can reduce anxiety and increase enthusiasm for the use of video by describing clear boundaries within which teacher professional learning will occur.

Walk the Talk

If superintendents, principals, coaches, and other educational leaders want to encourage others to use video, then one of the most powerful things they can do is to use it themselves. When superintendents record presentations to improve their presentation skills, or principals record meetings to see how they can be more encouraging and efficient, they are powerfully demonstrating the value of video. Furthermore, when leaders use video to improve, there is a very good chance they will learn something important.

Go Slow to Go Fast

Instructional leaders feel a lot of pressure to improve student learning and well-being instantly, and that pressure can lead them to push for the use of video too quickly. If leaders introduce video carelessly, teachers may resent and resist it, especially when they don't understand that it is primarily a tool they can use to meet their goals for themselves and their students. Quick fixes almost always inhibit deep change (Senge, 1990).

We suggest video be introduced with care, with principals and coaches using it as a tool to get better at their work. We also suggest coaches and administrators start with the people in the school who are highly respected. When the informal leaders in a school choose to use video, others often do it, too.

Using Video During Teacher Evaluation and Coaching

In *Focus on Teaching* (Knight, 2014), Jim describes a simple process principals and teachers can use to improve the teacher evaluation process through the use of video. First, principal and teacher should meet to discuss the evaluation tool. The master form we have included in this book is one example of such a tool. During their preliminary conversation, the principal and teacher should go through every item on the evaluation form to ensure that they both agree on the meaning of each kind of data described and what each kind of data looks like in practice. Then, the principal should visit the teacher's class at the time she would ordinarily use for an observation visit, video record the lesson, and share the video with the partnering teacher. Following this, both principal and teacher should watch the video on their own using the evaluation form and then complete it. Finally, principal and teacher should get together to discuss their analysis of the video, concluding their conversation with the teacher identifying a goal for improvement.

Chad Harnisch, a principal in Wisconsin, integrated video with teacher evaluation. For Chad, "Having the video as a snapshot in time of what actually happened in the classroom gave us a discussion that was rooted in the 'real' as opposed to what I think I may have experienced. Our conversation starts from the same place—this is what we saw on tape" (Knight, 2014, p. 129).

Video also plays a central role in instructional coaching. As an instructional coach from Noblesville, Indiana, told us, using video shifted the conversation to what the teacher was doing for their students, not what the coach personally thought (Knight, 2014, p. 44).

After conducting more than two decades of research on instructional coaching, Jim and his research colleagues in Kansas have identified a deceptively simple three-stage instructional coaching process that often incorporates video: *the Impact Cycle* (Knight, 2018).

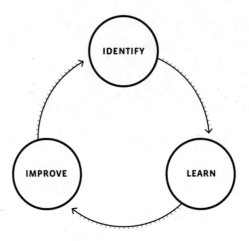

In this process, coaches use video at in the Identify stage to help teachers get a clear picture of reality. During the Learn stage, coaches often use video to create libraries of videos depicting teachers using strategies effectively, so other teachers can watch them and learn. Finally, during the Improve stage, teachers and coaches use video to monitor student progress toward the goal so teachers can review how they are implementing a strategy. (Chapter 4 contains an extended explanation of the Impact Cycle.)

Research Framework

Whenever possible, observations should be grounded in research. However, if observers only look for types of data that have been validated by empirical evidence, important variables might be missed. Our students need our best practices now—they cannot wait. It is impractical to ask educators to comb the existing literature for the latest evidence-based practices. For this reason, we have written this book with three mutually supportive lines of research in mind: theory, practice, and empirical research.

THEORY

Education is guided by theoretical frameworks for reading development, instructional sequences, service delivery models, and so on. These theories give rise to observable components of instruction—moving beyond theory into the reality of teacher–student learning interactions. Theory tells us what we might expect to occur in these interactions and what to look for: teacher actions, student engagement, lesson structures, classroom resources, and so on. We will share some of these important theories throughout the text. However, theory alone does not tell us about the reality you face daily.

PRACTICE

To make theory actionable, the second source of research has a practical or pragmatic foundation. Collectively, we have spent more than 50 years conducting formal and informal action research in real classrooms all across the country. We collaborate with a host of school partners, including teachers, learning specialists, instructional coaches, administrators, parents, and, of course, students. Our range of experiences include private and public, parochial and charter, elementary and secondary institutions, those with 60 students and those with 100,000 students.

These partnerships help surface critical instructional components for observation—some that fit established theories and others that are based on emerging evidence—to support student learning on a daily basis. We will share the voices of some these partners throughout the text so you can see yourself in these practices.

EMPIRICAL RESEARCH

Finally, as researchers ourselves, we rely heavily on interdisciplinary empirical literature. We read broadly in fields of education, special education, school psychology, speech and language pathology, educational leadership, and more. To know us is to know we have a shared reading challenge: We are constantly adding to each other's reading lists—from books to journals to research reports! At every opportunity, we have attempted to link each of the *Data Rules* practices to as robust a literature as possible. We have searched university databases, previewed thousands of articles, and coded (and recoded) to provide clarity about what, why, and how to observe these practices. Moreover, we have examined teacher, student, and staff actions, identified examples and nonexamples of practices, and, when possible, provided illustrations to bring these practices to life.

By linking theory, practice, and empirical research, we have endeavored to surface the most powerful, practical, and high-impact practices for improving outcomes for students. Our research has identified the following as critical components of impactful teaching:

- » Student engagement, measured through time on task, experience sampling, exit tickets, and surveys
- » Instructional and noninstructional time
- » The Engagement-Time Index (a global measure combining time on task and instructional time)
- » Teacher vs. student talk
- » Ratio of interaction (describing, reinforcing and correcting comments)
- » Correcting students (observing for consistency)
- » Student behavior (disruptions, respectful interactions)
- » Questions (type, kind, and level)
- » Student responses (opportunity, variety, correctness)
- » Teacher clarity
- » Formative assessment

Upcoming Chapters

Chapter 2: The 10 Data Rules

Data should foster hope, be chosen and gathered by the teacher when possible, be objective, valid, reliable and mutually understood, gathered frequently, easy to understand, and based on empirical evidence.

Chapter 3: Talking About Data

The most valuable conversations about data occur in psychologically safe contexts where people effectively listen, ask questions, and provide appropriate feedback. Effective data conversations are not one-directional; they are dialogical, with data serving as a third point for conversation.

Chapter 4: The Impact Cycle

Data stand at the heart of the universal coaching cycle we refer to as the Impact Cycle. This chapter provides an overview of the Identify, Learn, and Improve stages of the Impact Cycle and offers a description of how data are used at each stage of the cycle.

Chapter 5: Engagement

Behavioral engagement data reveal, in various ways, what students are doing (how they behave) during learning. Kinds of data to be discussed include time on task, disruptions, noninstructional time, responses to questions, and incivility. The chapter also includes a description of the Engagement-Time Index (ETI), a simple but powerful way to sum up behavioral engagement in a single number.

Chapter 6: Achievement

Assessing student achievement involves addressing a number of questions discussed in this chapter. First, what do we mean by "knowledge"—is it content, procedural, or conceptual? Second, what kind of learning is occurring—is it acquisition, connection, or transfer? Third, how do we unpack what students need to learn? Finally, what data tools can educators use to assess student learning?

Chapter 7: Teaching

After teachers set goals, they need to make changes that help them hit the goals. This chapter contains descriptions of several kinds of data related to how teachers interact with students, including how teachers ask questions and the ratio of teacher talk to student talk.

Chapter 8: Putting It All Together

Different people in different roles use data differently. This chapter describes how the different kinds of data discussed in this book can be integrated by principals, coaches, and teachers to foster better student learning and well-being.

Special Features of This Book

LEARNING MAPS

Each chapter begins with a learning map depicting the key ideas in the chapter and how those key ideas are connected. Readers can get a good overview of the book by simply reviewing the learning maps at the start of each chapter.

RESEARCH SUMMARIES

Chapters 5, 6, and 7 contain brief summaries of the research on the particular kind of data being discussed. Additionally, there are QR Codes and URLs linking to an extensive list of the literature on the kind of data being discussed. We have designed this book to be easy to use, but we also recognize the importance of explaining how research informs what and why we are including certain ideas and practices. For those who want to cut to the chase and start observing, the book should give you what you need. For those who want a detailed discussion of the research, the lists of the available literature will meet that need.

SIMPLE AND CLEAR DESCRIPTIONS

We want this book to be put into action, so we have worked with our editors to write in a way that is simple, clear, and easy to comprehend. Also, we have partnered with the Instructional Coaching Group's director of design, Chase Christensen, to create a book that is easily actionable. If we've done our job well, you should find this book very easy to use.

DATA FORMS

Throughout the book we have included data forms that observers can download to gather data in the classroom. They are designed so that they are easy to write on if uploaded to tablets and used with digital notetaking apps. Additionally, the content of each form is based on feedback by educators on how to make them more powerful and easier to use.

CHECKLISTS

We have included checklists that describe the essential characteristics of each kind of data discussed to make it easier for readers to learn how to gather data reliably. The checklists may be used by individuals who are practicing how to gather data or by teams of observers who are collaborating to increase the reliability of their observations.

TO SUM UP

Each chapter concludes with a summary of the main points in the chapter.

MAKING IT REAL

This section draws connections between the chapter's content and the work done by students, teachers, coaches, and administrators so that everyone can see how to apply the chapter's content.

GOING DEEPER

This section introduces resources (mostly books) readers can explore to extend their knowledge of the ideas and strategies discussed in the chapter.

To Sum Up
____

This chapter was largely about the central role data play in our lives and our schools. Three main topics were addressed.

1. DATA CONVERSATIONS ARE IMPORTANT BECAUSE:

» Most people don't have a clear picture of reality; data help them see more of what happens in their classrooms.

» Data are essential for motivation.

» Data are essential for goal setting.

» Data offer a way to monitor progress toward established goals.

2. FOR DATA TO BE EFFECTIVE, WE NEED TO BE ABLE TO SEE THEM:

» Video is more likely to be embraced when there is trust, choice, intrinsic motivation, boundaries, when leaders "walk the talk" by recording themselves, and when people "go slow to go fast."

» Video can accelerate professional learning during coaching and evaluation.

» Video recordings are used as points of departure for dialogue about data.

3. RESEARCH SHOULD PROVIDE THE BACKBONE FOR DISCUSSING DATA:

» Teachers need to understand the evidence in support of data use.

» Using the field-tested and refined forms in this book can provide objective data to empower instructional decision making.

Making It Real

Students

When students have a voice in their learning, they are more likely to be engaged and achieve. For that reason alone, asking students to share their perspective on their experiences in class is important. Students also provide very valuable data. Data-gathering tools such as exit tickets, surveys, and interviews can help teachers understand whether or not students feel connected to school, feel psychologically safe, and are engaged and learning.

Teachers

Learning how to gather and analyze data is one of the most important skills for any educator. Teacher professional development, including preservice, inservice, and coaching, should provide the support teachers need so that they can craft assessments that clearly identify what students need to learn, what students already know, and whether or not they are learning what they need. Additionally, teachers need to learn how to assess whether students are feeling behaviorally, cognitively, or emotionally engaged. Finally, each of these measures helps inform teachers about what they might do to improve student learning and well-being.

Coaches

Data are essential for coaches as they partner with teachers to identify goals, monitor progress toward goals, and make adjustments as changes are implemented in the classroom. Consequently, coaches need to identify what data are most useful to gather and then become reliable at gathering it. Coaches should bear in mind that data are one way of measuring whether or not students are learning and experiencing well-being and that coaching is about changes in students, not about numbers. Coaches should always question whether the data they gather truly assess the achievement, behavior, or attitude they are supposed to assess.

Administrators

When people gather data, they must gather data reliably; otherwise, discussions about the data are not useful. This is especially true when a teacher's evaluation is tied to the data. For this reason, administrators must receive sufficient professional development and practice so that they can be certain that their observations are reliable. It is much better to provide too much professional development and practice to be absolutely certain that data gathering is reliable than to provide too little support, resulting in unreliable observations. Principals, indeed anyone gathering data, should engage in extended practice of gathering data by visiting classrooms or watching video with others and then comparing their findings until the results are consistently the same.

Additionally, administrators must work to create a culture of trust in schools (more on this in Chapter 3) so that data conversations are productive and helpful and lead to better learning and better lives for students.

 Going Deeper

As we were writing *Data Rules*, we found *Street Data* by Shane Safir and Jamila Dugan, a book packed with ideas, tools, and practices that any educator can use to get a clearer picture of reality, set goals, and monitor progress. What we found most helpful, however, was that it clearly makes the case that data can help us see all students more clearly, a central theme of our book. Finally, *Street Data* contains descriptions of many methods that help us put that goal into practice.

The Data Coach's Guide to Improving Learning for All Students (2008) by Nancy Love, Katherine Stiles, Susan Mundry, and Kathyrn diRanna is the classic book on data and coaching.

◦━◦ PART ONE

CONVERSATIONS ABOUT DATA

THE 10 DATA RULES

are about

Effectively using data for professional learning

Hope

by fostering

by tying them to

Professional learning

by ensuring they are

Chosen by the teacher

by being

Objective

by ensuring they are

Reliable

by being

Valid

by gathering data

Frequently

by having data gathered by

Teachers

by making them

Easy to gather

by using data

Validated by research

CHAPTER 2

THE 10 DATA RULES

This chapter provides an overview of the 10 rules that we believe should guide the use of data in schools. In many ways the Data Rules are the heart of this book, so we think this chapter is pretty important. But if you're pressed for time, you could just jump ahead and read the headings for each rule and skim the paragraphs to get an overview of the chapter. No judgment here if you skim it, but this might be a chapter to dive into.

CHAPTER RESOURCES

Access charts, diagrams, research, and resources from this chapter.

All models are wrong, but some are useful.

GEORGE BOX

A few years back, one of us sat in a school district meeting where administrators and educators talked about the latest student achievement results. The news was not good. Students' test scores hadn't shown any significant improvements over the past year, and, in fact, some scores had gone down. After sharing the disappointing results, the district leader turned to the teachers who were attending and said, "Look. You have to teach better. Our students deserve better, and what you've always done isn't good enough. Things have to change."

The administrator's desire to see improvement for students was well-intended, but the way he expressed it wasn't helpful. Almost all the teachers in the room were dedicated to working hard for children. They wanted students to achieve as much or more than anyone in the room, but they didn't know what they could do to increase their impact. If they knew what to change to reach more students, they would be doing it. The leader wanted to push teachers to improve, but most likely every teacher left the meeting unhappy, discouraged, and less open to change.

Meetings like this give data a bad name. Sharing low scores at the conclusion of the school year is discouraging for those who chose a career in teaching because they wanted to positively impact the lives of their students. But data don't have to be used in this way. Used effectively, data can foster hope and lead to positive improvements in students' learning and well-being. We've identified 10 Data Rules educators can use to guide their use of data. The rules are described below.

Rule #1: Data Should Foster Hope

─────

University of Kansas researchers Rick Snyder (2003) and Shane Lopez (2014) have described three elements that are necessary for hope. People who have hope, the researchers have explained, have (a) a preferred future or goal; that is, something to hope for; (b) pathways to that goal; that is, some possible ways of meeting the goal; and (c) agency, a belief that they can hit the goal if they follow the pathway.

When used correctly, data foster hope. Data can help teachers identify a preferred future by shining a light on particular aspects of student learning and behavior. When teachers review data on students' emotional engagement, for example, they will know more about their students' current reality and they can use that knowledge to set goals related to students' emotional engagement. Once teachers start making changes in their classroom to increase students' engagement or achievement, they can gather data to monitor progress toward the goal. Used effectively, therefore, data help teachers (a) identify what they hope for, (b) measure the effectiveness of the pathway to the goal, and (c) build agency by showing what progress is being made. In short, data don't have to feel like a punishment. Data can foster hope.

Rule #2: Data Should Be Tied to Professional Learning

─────

For teachers to have hope, they need to use data to identify a pathway that will enable them to move toward their goal, and then they need to use data to monitor progress until the goal is met. If teachers don't see a pathway to their goal, they won't feel hope.

Professional learning helps teachers identify and follow pathways to their preferred futures. Often such learning takes place when educators partner with coaches to move through a coaching cycle. We have spent more than two decades developing, refining, and validating a coaching cycle we refer to as the Impact Cycle (Knight, 2018), described in detail in Chapter 4. Although aspects of the Impact Cycle can be employed by teachers for self-reflection or by principals in partnership with teachers, the cycle is most frequently implemented by teachers with coaches. Chapter 4 contains an overview of the three stages of the cycle—Identify, Learn, and Improve— as well as an explanation of how those stages can be adapted for use by individuals, teams, or instructional coaches.

Rule #3: Data Should Be Chosen by the Teacher

There are many kinds of data that are not chosen by the teacher. State tests, for example, are outside the control of teachers and school leaders, and, like it or not, schools and teachers in the United States and other countries are often assessed by that data. Also, in most settings, teacher evaluation involves data that are not chosen by the teacher even though there might be great advantages to involving teachers in identifying the standards for evaluation.

When it comes to professional learning, however, there are many reasons why teachers should identify what data will be gathered to monitor progress to goals. First, each classroom is a distinct collection of a wide range of students guided by a unique teacher. Consequently, the most relevant data in one setting might not be as relevant and helpful in another setting. Also, the person who knows the most about the students and the teacher is, of course, the teacher. For these reasons, teachers are often best positioned to identify the data to be gathered for their professional learning.

A central assumption of this book is that teachers are professionals who use their professional judgment to make decisions about what happens in their classrooms. We talk about professional development (the learning activities teachers experience) and professional learning (the growth and transformation that is the result of effective professional development), but professional development and professional learning are only possible when we treat teachers as professionals. By telling teachers what their goals will be and what data will be covered, we are treating teachers more like workers on an assembly line than professionals. Our students deserve professionals teaching them, but we won't have professional teachers unless they have many opportunities to use their professional judgment.

Change happens from the inside out, not from the outside in. People are motivated by their own goals. If we want people to be motivated to change, we need to encourage them to set their own goals and identify their own data. Human beings are very skilled at nodding their heads yes and not changing, and if we want people to commit rather than comply, we are wise to encourage them to set their own goals.

A teacher, of course, may not know what data to gather. When this is the case, a coach who understands the kinds of data described in this book can be very helpful. A knowledgeable coach can suggest possible kinds of data that a teacher might choose. However, this should be a nuanced conversation. The coach should interact in a way that ensures that teachers choose the data while also clearly describing different types of data. A coach might ask a teacher for permission to share data, thereby demonstrating respect for the teacher. Then the coach could offer choices, saying something like, "When teachers have been interested in increasing engagement, they often look at increasing time on task, decreasing disruptions, or increasing instructional time by shortening how long transitions take or looking at how students respond to questions. Will any of these forms of data help you see if you are hitting your goal?"

Rule #4: Data Should Be Objective

Data can be gathered either objectively or subjectively. When something is subjective, according to the *Oxford English Dictionary* (OED; oed.com), it is "related to the thinking subject, proceeding from, or taking place within the subject, having its source in the mind." Subjective data, then, are based on the thoughts in someone's minds about what they are observing. When something is objective, on the other hand, it is based on something "external to the mind." That is, objective data are "the actual facts, not colored by the feelings or opinions of the writer" (OED).

How we talk about data varies, therefore, depending on whether the data are subjective or objective. For example, someone who gathers subjective data might say, "You asked some good questions, but I don't think your students were engaged." In contrast, someone who gathers objective data might say, "You asked 17 closed questions and 4 open questions, and 5 of your 27 students answered the questions." A coach gathering objective data might even put tallies on a seating chart to show which students answered questions or note the cognitive level of each student's responses. Objective data are the soul of providing authentic feedback that can be valued by all parties involved in the coaching conversation.

There are several problems with using subjective data. First, our perceptions of reality are imperfectly filtered through our perceptual errors and defense mechanisms. If a teacher turns to an observer and says, "That's not what happened in the class," they usually are correct at least from their perspective.

Another problem with subjective data is that by virtue of their personal nature—they involve my opinion of what is happening in your classroom—subjective comments can trigger defensiveness on the part of the person receiving the feedback. When someone asks, "Would you like to hear my opinion on how you teach?" most of us, I suspect, if we were being really honest, would be inclined to say no. The reality is that our advice isn't as good as we think, and people don't want to hear it as much as we think (see *Advice Trap* [Stanier, 2020] for an excellent discussion of the problems with the so-called Advice Giving Habit [AGH]).

The difference between subjective and objective data becomes clear if you watch the Winter Olympics. During speed skating, for example, when the race is over, the winner is the person who crosses the line the fastest. Assuming everyone is judged to have raced fairly, whoever makes it to the finish line in the shortest amount of time goes home with the gold. Consequently, there are very few controversies about who was the fastest during a speed skating race. This is how objective data work. There's no opinion involved; the data just are what they are.

During figure skating, however, the data are subjective and the story, therefore, is completely different. Figure skaters, or at least figure skating commentators, often criticize the way in which skaters are scored. Indeed, the fact that gold medals are handed out based on subjective opinion has led to numerous arguments and controversies. During the 2002 Winter Olympics, in fact, Canadians Jamie Salé and David Pelletier were not awarded their gold medals until several days after the competition after many figure skating experts had criticized the subjective scores offered by judges.

Once selected, objective data are not personal—they are factual. When I gather and share reliable, objective data, my opinion doesn't guide the conversation; I am just reporting the facts. In contrast, subjective data, by definition, always involve my opinion. Conversations about my opinion can turn the focus away from what happened in a classroom and toward whether or not my opinion is correct. For this reason, we suggest educators gather objective data. This book offers descriptions of dozens of examples of objective data anyone can gather.

Rule #5: Data Should Be Reliable and Mutually Understood

When researchers talk about reliable data, they mean that the data are consistent regardless of who gathers them. Thus, four different researchers observing the same classroom will produce the same results with little variation if their data gathering is reliable. This kind of reliability is also important outside of research situations, such as when administrators gather data for teacher evaluation. Most teachers would feel frustrated if two administrators gave them contrary evaluative feedback based on differing interpretations of a teacher-evaluation tool.

Reliability is a bit different in coaching situations. What matters there is that the coach and teacher have the same understanding of the data. For example, if a teacher wants to decrease the number of disruptions by increasing the ratio of interaction, it is important that the teacher trusts the coach's data.

One way to increase mutual understanding is for the coach and teacher to create a T-chart that describes examples and nonexamples of data. For example, a T-chart for time on task (explained in Chapter 5) might include "listening to teacher during direct instruction" on the example side of the chart and "engaging in side conversations" on the nonexample side.

TIME ON TASK T-CHART

What it is	What it isn't
Listening to direct instruction	Having side conversations
Using technology for learning	Playing with technology or social media
Participating in classroom discussion	Bothering other students
Participating in group work	Sleeping or nodding off
Participating in partner talk	Out of seat without permission
Doing activities such as practice, test taking, and so on	Not taking out materials
Taking notes	Doing other activities such as reading or homework for another class
Completing work as requested in class	Texting

Source: From *The Definitive Guide to Instructional Coaching* by Jim Knight, 2021.

Rule #6: Data Should Be Valid

——

Data are valid when they measure what they are intended to measure. For example, asking someone to complete a multiple-choice test on bicycle riding would not be as valid as watching someone ride, or fail to ride, a bike. It's the same in the classroom. Teachers and observers need to make sure that the data they gather are actually measuring what students are supposed to be learning.

Sometimes observers must settle for less reliable data in order to get more valid data. For example, data that can be gathered reliably, such as time on task (explained in Chapter 5), can tell us whether students look engaged, but they don't tell us what is going on in students' minds. A student who looks like she is thinking about a writing task might actually be thinking, "Wouldn't it be cool if Taylor Swift moved in next door?" To get a better understanding of how students are thinking, teachers might find it more helpful to ask students to self-report on their level of engagement than using time on task, even though we cannot know for sure how accurately students are reporting.

Similarly, different types of assessments are more valid for some kinds of learning than others. Giving students quizzes or tests might be valid for measuring whether students have acquired knowledge, for example, but assessing how well students transfer skills might be more validly measured through rubrics. All data are imperfect; what matters is that we gather data that give us the most useful insight into what we are assessing.

Rule #7: Data Should Be Gathered Frequently

——

Imagine a GPS that only told you when you had arrived at your destination. No "recalculating," just the message "you have arrived" when you get home. Such a tool clearly wouldn't be very helpful. When we're headed toward a destination, we need to know if we are taking the right route.

The same thing can be said for change. When we try out a new strategy, we need to know if we are on the right path or if we must make adjustments along the way. Experts on the personal experience of change describe the nonlinear progress of change in different ways. For example, Prochaska and his colleagues (1994) write that setbacks are an inevitable part of change and that "the average successful self-changer recycles several times" (p. 47).

Brian Moran and Michael Lennington (2013) suggest another model for under-standing change. Adapting Don Kelley and Daryl Connor's *Emotional Cycle of Change* (1979), Moran and Lennington describe change as a movement from uninformed optimism to informed pessimism, and if everything goes well, eventually to "success and fulfillment," which sometimes runs through "the valley of despair" (p. 72).

Similarly, Michael Fullan, after decades of studying educational change initiatives around the globe, writes that people attempting to change usually experience an "implementation dip" (2001, p. 41). That is, we begin change filled with enthusiasm, but we quickly realize that adjustments have to be made. Seth Godin even wrote a book about this change pattern, which he named, appropriately, *The Dip* (2007).

What this all means is that data need to be gathered frequently if they are going to be helpful. We suggest data be gathered at least weekly. As we try new practices, we need to know whether or not those practices are working. Gathering achievement data once or twice a semester, or even less frequently, say only at the end of the year, and expecting them to help guide instructional improvement, is a bit like trying to find our way home with a GPS that only tells us when we have arrived at our destination.

Most strategies need to be refined, adapted, or changed to have the desired impact. Teachers need to identify what they can measure weekly that shows progress towards improvement in state scores. A teacher interested in seeing improvement in students' scores on the Six-Traits writing assessment, for example, can create a rubric that they can use weekly to assess student performance on one or all of the traits. Frequently gathered data can be like a crystal ball educators can consult to forecast results.

Once educators have identified the data to be gathered, they can still make modifications so the data become more valid. Often, for example, teachers realize that a rubric must be changed to assess student performance more accurately. Learning is a living experience, not static, and the data that are at the heart of learning may have to be adapted to be more effective.

Rule #8: Data Should Be Gathered by the Teacher

———

Even when data are objective, educators' defense mechanisms (listed in Chapter 1) may make it difficult for them to see or accept data that have been gathered by an observer in their classroom. For that reason, we suggest teachers gather their own data, when possible, since teachers who analyze and gather their own data are more likely to accept and value the data.

The easiest way for teachers to gather data on what is happening in their classroom is to video record their lessons. Not all types of data can be reliably measured by watching a video recording of a lesson, but many of the kinds of data described in this book (including questions, opportunities to respond, number of different students responding, teacher talk vs. student talk, etc.) can be very reliably gathered. An added bonus is that observers who use video can go back and rewatch segments of a lesson to better understand exactly what happened. When the observer is the teacher herself, those data can especially lead to powerful learning.

Rule #9: Data Should Be Easy to Gather and Review

———

Teaching is time-intensive, complicated, emotionally complex work, and a perfectly crafted rubric that takes hours of time and thinking to implement may easily be tossed aside as being too difficult to use. When teachers decide what data to gather, they should consider whether the assessment is worth the effort. The best assessments, like the best strategies, are powerful and easy, revealing great insight into students' well-being or learning while also being easy to administer.

Rule #10: Data Should Be Validated by Research

Finally, conversations about data are not productive if the data being gathered have little impact on student achievement or well-being. We suggest that observers prioritize data that align instructional practices validated by research with areas of desired improvement in student outcomes. In this way, data are more likely to be useful when making instructional decisions, with the added benefit of being more efficient at yielding desired results. Moreover, when data are validated by research, teacher confidence grows, helping them be more likely to experiment with innovative methods to meet the evolving needs of their students.

 # To Sum Up

---

This chapter described 10 Data Rules that will improve how effectively data are used.

Data should...

» Rule #1: Foster Hope

» Rule #2: Be Tied to Professional Learning

» Rule #3: Be Chosen by the Teacher

» Rule #4: Be Objective

» Rule #5: Be Reliable and Mutually Understood

» Rule #6: Be Valid

» Rule #7: Be Gathered Frequently

» Rule #8: Be Gathered by the Teacher

» Rule #9: Be Easy to Gather and Review

» Rule #10: Be Validated by Research

Making It Real

Students

Students are the great untapped resource for professional learning. Every classroom is filled with students who are watching the teacher and who can give feedback, yet that opportunity for feedback is frequently overlooked. While we can't count on student data to be reliable, as is the case with anyone offering subjective self-report data, student comments can still be very helpful. When teachers involve students in their professional learning goals and ask students for feedback, they often gain valuable insights into their students' experiences, and students who are asked to provide feedback often feel validated by a teacher who values what they have to say.

Teachers

Many of the kinds of data described in this book can be gathered, analyzed, and used by teachers for professional learning. However, in some cases, the data will need to be drawn from a video of a lesson. The easiest data to gather are exit tickets and other self-reports from students. Teachers gathering data on their teaching may find it helpful to record themselves teaching and listen to the recording as they drive home, for example—though no doubt all of us have had days when the last thing we want to do is relive a lesson we've just taught. In that case, saving the data to review prior to creating the next lesson plan ensures accuracy of what occurred and brings objectivity for teachers reflecting on what to do next for students. Data, such as the number of students responding to questions or teacher talk vs. student talk, are fairly easy to estimate while listening to or watching a lesson. But in other cases, such as observing student engagement, a teacher will need a coach's help to gather data. Indeed, coaches can be a big help to teachers in almost all cases.

Coaches

All the data described in this book can be gathered by coaches; indeed, coaches need to be highly proficient at gathering data. Using data is the way for teachers to set goals, measure progress, and, ultimately, build agency. For these reasons, applying the Data Rules and gathering data are essential skills for instructional coaches.

There are many things coaches can do to become proficient at data gathering. For example, groups of coaches can practice observing lessons by watching video, gathering data, comparing notes, and discussing what they observed in the video. Sometimes there is value in going back through the video minute by minute and discussing what everyone has noted. Coaches can also ask teachers for permission to observe classrooms in pairs. Then after the class, coaches can discuss what they observed.

Administrators

We believe that the Data Rules can help administrators bring about more significant improvements for students. When administrators advocate for data that foster hope, are identified and gathered by teachers, are valid and reliable, are easy to gather, and are frequently gathered, we believe they will see real improvement. Ultimately, the Data Rules foster professional and classroom learning—and learning, of course, is what it's all about.

 # Going Deeper

Two books are particularly relevant to this chapter. The first is Shane Lopez's *Making Hope Happen* (2013). We are big believers in hope theory, and Lopez's book is the most accessible source on the topic. Lopez first defines hope and its components and then suggests what we can do to increase hope in others and ourselves. We think this is important reading for any educator.

The second book is *Changing for Good* (1994) by James Prochaska, John Norcross, and Carlo DiClemente. A classic study of the personal experience of change, the two big

ideas in the book are: (a) change happens in stages—precontemplation, contempla-
tion, preparation, action, maintenance, termination—and (b) change is nonlinear. In
other words, we do not move through a set series of stages of change, we move back
and forth, and it often takes several attempts before we are able to make a change.
We find this view of change oddly comforting as we struggle with our own changes or
partner with others who are trying to change. Also, the authors' discussion of precontemplation—our tendency not to see that we need to change—provides a clear
argument for why we need to gather data on what happens when we do our work.

TALKING ABOUT DATA

is about

---

having positive, productive
conversations about data

---

*by
applying*

*by
considering*

*by
applying*

Data Rules

Identity
Factors

Partnership
Principles

- Equality
- Choice
- Voice
- Dialogue
- Reflection
- Praxis
- Reciprocity

CHAPTER 3

TALKING ABOUT DATA

This chapter is about how to have better conversations about data by embracing the Partnership Principles (Knight, 2021) and by using the communication skills, habits, and behaviors that result from translating the Partnership Principles into action. If you know a lot about the Partnership Principles and better conversation skills and habits, you might consider skipping this chapter, but the information here is directly related to talking about data.

CHAPTER RESOURCES

Access charts, diagrams, research, and resources from this chapter.

Be brave enough to start a conversation that matters.

MARGARET WHEATLEY

Recently, one of us talked with a new assistant principal about his experiences in his first year as an administrator. He was excited to have an opportunity to do good work for teachers and students. He hoped that one day he would lead his own school. The only part of the job that he really didn't like was talking about teacher evaluation data. All his experiences in that area, he confessed, had pretty much been negative. "The way I see it," he said, "when I talk with teachers about their evaluation, if the teacher doesn't get angry or cry, it's been a good conversation." That's a pretty low bar for human interaction.

We don't know how our new administrator was taught to discuss data, but unsuccessful data conversations often follow the same pattern. An observer visits a teacher's classroom and gathers data. Then the observer meets with the teacher to tell the teacher what they did right and wrong. After reviewing the data, the observer tells the teacher what to do to be better.

There is power in such a simple story, but it overlooks the reality that when it comes to change, whether we recognize it or not, people have a choice. As every teacher knows all too well, you can't force people to learn. Most people, children and adults, are skilled at nodding their heads yes and not changing at all. Real change involves a choice. Telling people what to do might get compliance at best, but it won't get commitment.

Talking about data doesn't have to be like that. Our main point in this book is that data conversations can be positive, interesting, even life-giving conversations that foster hope and improvements in teaching and, ultimately, in student learning and well-being. There is a lot we can do to have better conversations about data. That is what this chapter is all about.

Why Do Data Conversations Fail?
———

The Data Rules, described in Chapter 2, shine a light on many actions that can improve how we talk about data. For example, data should be shared as part of a professional learning process, such as coaching, that helps teachers identify and monitor pathways to their goals. Data should be valid, reliable, and mutually under-stood if a conversation is going to be worthwhile. Further, objective data usually lead to better conversations than subjective data. When teachers set their own goals, perhaps in partnership with a coach, and then gather their own data, perhaps through the use of rubrics and checks for understanding or by reviewing video of the classroom, they usually find the experience more useful than listening to someone else's observations about data that they didn't choose themselves.

Identity

How we talk about data, whether with a colleague, coach, or as self-reflection, is just as important as following the Data Rules. When an observer shares data that suggest instruction isn't working, teachers often take it personally. When people take things personally, when they feel that their identity is threatened, they often shift the conversation from what the data show to defending themselves. As Douglas Stone and Sheila Heen write in *Thanks for the Feedback* (2015), feedback that trig-gers thoughts about our identity can [cause] us to feel "overwhelmed, threatened, ashamed, or off balance … our identity—our sense of who we are—[can] come undone" (p. 17).

In our work, we've found four identify factors that need to be considered during data conversations. Each factor is important because its absence can upset a potentially helpful conversation about data.

FACTOR 1. GOOD CHARACTER. If our way of interacting leads others to believe we are saying that they are immoral in some way (you don't care about kids) or that they have a character flaw of some sort (you should work harder on your lesson planning), they will defend their character rather than consider the issues raised by data.

FACTOR 2: COMPETENCE. When people perceive that we are saying they are incompetent, whether that is our intent or not, they will likely take issue with the suggestion and want to spend the conversation defending themselves.

FACTOR 3: ACCEPTANCE. People want to feel accepted by others. Put most positively, people want to feel loved by others. Put more negatively, people don't want to be rejected by others. In fact, people don't even want to feel rejected by people that they might reject. When people do not feel accepted by someone sharing data, they may struggle to focus on whatever the person giving the feedback is saying.

FACTOR 4: CONTROL. People want to have some control over their lives. As a result, telling people what to do is a very ineffective way of motivating them to change. What research has shown us about human motivation is that while telling people what to do may lead to compliance (people do what they're told to do because they want to keep their jobs), it won't lead to commitment (people doing all they can to have a positive impact on others).

Worthwhile conversations should increase, not decrease, competence. The best conversations occur when all parties feel heard, when back-and-forth shared thinking helps people identify more effective strategies or make better plans because everyone's brain is involved. The best conversations are positive, energizing, and worthwhile. We call that kind of interaction a partnership conversation.

The Partnership Approach to Talking About Data

For close to two decades, Jim has been studying how conversations either foster or inhibit learning. What he has found (Knight, 2000) is that people learn best when they learn in partnership with people who value them and their ideas, who don't try to control them, who ask great questions, and who listen and think with them. Jim describes these conversations as embodying a partnership approach.

When Jim studied the partnership approach, he contrasted it with a directive approach and found that the partnership approach produced significantly more engagement, happiness, learning, and higher expectation to implement (four times more). In short, when people felt that their opinions mattered, they got a lot more out of their learning experiences (Knight, 2000).[1]

Based on this research, Jim created a set of principles to describe the partnership approach, but over the years we have found that those principles, by themselves, do not fully describe the approach. Partnership is a set of beliefs and a set of actions. These actions and beliefs, described below, create the conditions for positive, energizing, helpful conversations about many things in life, including data.

THE PARTNERSHIP PRINCIPLES

Equality

Choice

Voice

Dialogue

Reflection

Praxis

Reciprocity

---

[1]You can read the paper describing the study at https://www.instructionalcoaching.com/resources/research.

Equality

The principle: I don't believe any person or group is more valuable than any other, and I recognize and honor the dignity of every individual.

WHAT IT LOOKS LIKE

Equality is both a global belief about humanity and a personal way of interacting with others. To accept the principle of equality is to believe, as is written in the United Nations' Declaration of Human Rights, that "all human beings are born free and equal in dignity and rights" and that "recognition of the inherent dignity and of the equal and inalienable rights of all members of the human family is the foundation of freedom, justice and peace in the world" (www.un.org).

Believing that others are as important as we are shapes how we interact with others. First off, if we believe in equality, we shouldn't interrupt others. When we interrupt, our actions are saying "my voice is more important than yours," or simply "I'm more important than you." Interruption is a power move; it is a way of taking control of a conversation.

You can see the damage that interruptions can do by watching a news program where the interviewer holds a view of reality that is different from that of the person being interviewed. When this is the case, chances are the interviewer will interrupt throughout the conversation—sometimes five or more interruptions in a minute— to stop the other person from saying something that contradicts the interviewer's world view, to stop cogent arguments, or to maintain control. If we believe others are as important as we are, we shouldn't interrupt them.

Another way to demonstrate equality is by refusing to moralistically judge others. As Marshall Rosenberg has written (2003), "Moralistic judgments ... imply wrongness or badness on the part of people who don't act in harmony with our values. Such judgments are reflected in language: 'The problem with you is that you're too selfish.' 'She's lazy ...' 'It's inappropriate.' Blame, insults, put-downs, labels, criticism, comparisons, and diagnoses are all forms of judgment" (p. 15). Moralistic judgment is a learning and intimacy killer because those who feel judged tend to either defend themselves or stop listening. We usually don't seek help from people who roll their eyes (a sign of annoyance, exasperation, or disbelief) when they talk about our needs.

When an observer makes moralistically judgmental comments about a teacher's competence ("How could you allow the students to waste so much time?"), those words can damage morale, damage relationships, and decrease people's openness to collaboration. In other words, if you feel judged, you're less likely to be vulnerable and open during a conversation, and if you're not open and vulnerable, you're less likely to learn.

Stanford researcher Liz Wiseman's studies (2010) on what she calls *multipliers* and *diminishers* provide a framework for understanding why moralistically judgmental comments inhibit change. When observers communicate moralistic judgment ("you need to do better than this") along with data, those being judged often feel diminished, experiencing less self-efficacy, less energy for improvement. On the other hand, when data are communicated affirmatively ("time on task is 65%, but I know that together we can quickly get it up to our goal of 90%"), those being affirmed while receiving data often feel empowered, experience higher self-efficacy, and have more energy for improvement.

What matters here is that the conversations are grounded in data and that they are authentic. A rose-colored glasses approach to data doesn't lead to change. We can't improve on reality by avoiding it. But when observers share realistic, valid data while also communicating their belief in others, real change can happen.

QUESTIONS: Do I see myself as superior to my colleagues—like a parent talks to a child—or do I see others as equals? Do I interrupt? Do I moralistically judge others?

Choice

The principle: I communicate in a way that acknowledges the professional discretion of others by ensuring that they make most decisions about their professional practice.

We sometimes show a DocMorris commercial in our workshops to illustrate what we have found to be true about the personal experience of change. In the short video, a man who appears to be in his 70s starts a personal fitness routine to improve his upper-body strength. Each morning, at 6:30, he wakes up to exercise with a kettlebell even though his nosy neighbor thinks he is being ridiculous. After much exercise, the man goes to his daughter's home to give his granddaughter a Christmas present. Her face lights up when she opens the present and finds a star for the top of the Christmas tree. Then the man lifts her up so she can place the star on top of the tree, and we see why he has been working out so diligently. His hard work has paid off in renewed strength. Touched by her father's action, the daughter looks at him with tears in her eye.

We have watched the commercial many times and noticed that the man in the commercial always places a picture of his granddaughter in front of him when he exercises. Each morning when he lifts the kettlebell, he puts the picture of his grand-daughter in front of him to stay motivated and focused. Indeed, the last shot of the commercial is the photograph sitting on the man's desk.

People are rarely motivated by others telling them what they have to do. Change happens from the inside out. Based on the literature on change and human moti-vation and our two and a half decades of studying instructional coaching, we have found that people only change when they have a strong personal reason to change and that such an emotional commitment to a goal is much more likely when people have a choice.

WHAT IT LOOKS LIKE

There are, of course, many things teachers do that are not choices. In most schools, for example, it probably wouldn't go over well if a teacher said, "I find I teach better after a couple glasses of Sauvignon Blanc, so I think I'll put a little wine cooler in my classroom." Anyone who works in a community will have their behavior shaped by the norms and expectations of that community. In a workplace like a school that means, for example, that teachers, whether they like them or not, have to implement districtwide initiatives—though those initiatives will be welcomed more enthusiasti-cally if the teachers have a say in them.

As every teacher knows all too well, you can't force people to learn or change. When leaders and coaches recognize these facts—that you can't force people to change, that change always involves a choice, that people usually only commit to goals they care about, those coaches and leaders have a better chance of creating the condi-tions necessary for people to learn, grow, and improve.

When people embrace the principle of choice, they don't see their job as fixing others or solving their problems. Rather, they see their job as creating conditions that enable others to independently set goals that matter, make plans to hit those goals, and consequently learn and grow. Such change agents use data to help others see and interpret their own reality and to monitor progress. The Impact Cycle (Knight, 2018), described in Chapter 4, is a process leaders and coaches can use to help teachers use their professional discretion to interpret data, set goals, and monitor progress until the goals are met.

QUESTION: Can I let go of control?

Voice

The principle: I want to hear what others have to say, and I communicate that clearly.

WHAT IT LOOKS LIKE

When Gallup surveyed over 1 million workers to identify what was most important in setting up employees to succeed, they found that one of the 12-most important things was for people to feel like their opinion mattered. As the Gallup researchers reported, "when employees feel they are involved in decisions, they take greater ownership for the outcomes" (2016, p. 336).

When we decide to embrace the principle of choice, the way we interact with others should show that we believe their opinions are important. The most obvious way to communicate that we value what others have to say is by carefully listening to them. Fortunately, effective listening is a skill that almost anyone can learn.

Good listening involves both internal and external factors. Internally, we need to make sure that our attention is mostly focused on what our conversation partner says. This can be challenging since most people talk slower than our brains move and we, therefore, can lose focus even during the most interesting conversations. Good listeners train themselves to stay focused by processing what the other person says without judgment, without making assumptions, without planning clever responses, or having mental arguments while supposedly listening to their conversation partners. Good listeners listen with open hearts, without assumptions, judgment, or "yeah, buts."

But staying focused on what our conversation partners say is just one part of good listening. When we listen effectively, we also communicate nonverbally that we are listening. This means that we turn toward our conversation partner, make an appropriate amount of eye contact, nod, and act in other ways that communicate we're listening. Additionally, good listeners don't interrupt, don't complete their conversation partners' sentences, don't suggest the word a person is trying to remember. Good listeners ask a question and then let their conversation partner answer.

QUESTION: Does my conversation partner know that I value what they have to say?

Dialogue

The principle: I believe conversations should consist of a back-and-forth exchange, with all parties hearing and responding to one another's opinions.

When two people come together as equals, when they listen to each other and explore ideas together without trying to control each other, they engage in a kind of conversation that might be called a dialogue. Such a conversation is characterized by mutual respect, and ideas move between those in the conversation so fluidly that it becomes hard to know who said what. During a dialogue people think together.

Unfortunately, too often, when people talk about data, only one person does the talking. During data conversations, what happens is often similar to what we described at the start of this chapter: An observer gathers data on a teacher, interprets the data, tells the teacher what the data mean, and then tells the teacher what to do to improve in an area of concern the observer found in the data. As illustrated in our comments on the principle of choice, a top-down model of interaction like this is rarely effective.

Harvard researchers Robert Kegan and Lisa Lahey (2001) identify two problematic assumptions that are implicit in top-down conversations:

> The first [assumption] is that the perspective of the feedback giver (let's call him the supervisor)—what he sees and thinks, his feedback—is right, is correct. An accompanying assumption is that there is only one correct answer. When you put these two assumptions together, they amount to

this: the supervisor has the one and only correct view of the situation. (We call this "the super vision assumption"; that is, the super-visor has super vision). (p. 128)

Top-down conversations often create resistance. As former MIT business theorist and psychologist Edgar Schein explains in his many influential books (see especially *Helping*, 2009), people who don't get the status they think they deserve rarely embrace the feedback they receive. If I perceive my conversation partner as putting himself one up on me and perceive myself as being put one down, odds are I will resist what my partner has to share. If I feel like I am always placed in the one-down position during data conversations, I may hold very low expectations for those conversations.

A dialogue is a different kind of conversation; it's a back-and-forth conversation between two or more people thinking together. The two and a half decades we've spent reading about dialogue[2] and studying learning conversations in schools have led us to identify six conditions for dialogue.

OPENNESS

We can't engage in dialogue unless we are open to hearing and processing what others say. Dialogue is back and forth. People who want to engage in dialogue need to have the courage, vulnerability, and emotional intelligence to open themselves to ideas that may contradict their beliefs and assumptions. In fact, one important reason for taking a dialogical approach is that it helps us see beyond our limited view of reality. We engage in dialogue most successfully when we approach others with curiosity, assuming there is always something more to learn.

PSYCHOLOGICAL SAFETY

Our opportunity to learn from others is significantly blocked if others don't feel comfortable telling us what they think. This is especially challenging since, as Harvard Leadership Professor Amy Edmondson writes, "not offering an idea is an invisible act" (2019, p. 46). Because we usually don't know when people choose to keep

---

[2]See Paulo Freire, *Pedagogy of the Oppressed* (2018), and William Isaacs, *Dialogue* (1999), for two different perspectives on dialogue that influenced our thinking, among others.

their ideas to themselves, we need to do all we can do to ensure that they feel safe sharing their ideas if we want to foster dialogue. This means we need to understand and regulate our emotions to ensure we give a quick negative response to a challenge comment that silences our conversation partner. Communicating appreciation to others also builds psychological safety for dialogue, especially when we communicate that we value others' ideas.

SHARING OUR IDEAS

Just as we won't have a dialogue if others don't share what they think, we won't have a dialogue if we don't share what we think. When we share ideas dialogically, we offer our ideas provisionally, saying something like, "Let me put this on the table and you tell me what you think." Dialogue involves balancing telling and asking. We share what we think, but at the same time, we encourage others to poke holes in our ideas so that, ultimately, we can see and learn more and act more effectively.

CONFIDENCE

Dialogue also requires that we approach others with confidence, not fear. We can be open to others' ideas, be vulnerable, and still be confident that the conversation we're about to have will be productive. This means that we must develop knowledge, skills, beliefs, and conversational procedures, such as the Impact Cycle described in Chapter 4, so that we can engage others from a solid footing. It also means that we approach others confident that they can succeed—seeing each person for what they can do in the future, not simply for what they are doing right now.

A dialogue is a conversation about a potentially better future, a constructive conversation that moves things forward. A dialogue about data, then, is a conversation that uses data as the point of departure for exploring what can lead to better learning and better well-being for students.

BENEVOLENCE

Dialogue is predicated on the belief that, as the popular phrase states, "together we can do more." We enter into dialogue focused on doing right, not being right. This requires that we choose to do what we can for the good of others rather than ourselves. So, when we discuss data with teachers, they know that we genuinely want what is best for them and their students. We should clearly communicate to teachers that we are on their side, that we believe in them, and that we want them to succeed.

TRUST

It is difficult to have a dialogical conversation with someone we don't trust, and many of the conditions described here will help build trust. Wanting to hear what others have to say, wanting what is best for our conversation partners, and being confident in ourselves and others lay the groundwork for trust. There are other actions we can take to build trust. Most important, perhaps, is to act in a "trustworthy" way. A trustworthy person is reliable, honest, transparent, and fair. If we speak the truth, do what we said we would do when we said we would, and adopt the other behaviors described here, we will make great strides toward creating trust and, ultimately, fostering dialogue.

Dialogue is often facilitated through the use of a third point or what Parker Palmer calls "third things" for dialogue (2004). According to Parker, we can promote dialogue and meaningful conversation by using third things to turn the focus of the conversation away from the people in the conversation and toward something external. This "thing" may be a poem, story, piece of music, or, more relevant to this chapter, data.

The idea is that when two or more people have a "third thing" to discuss, such as data, the focus turns away from the individuals and turns toward the thing, which is to say, the conversation becomes more back and forth or dialogical. In this way, dialogue melts away the coach's role as coach and the teacher's role as teacher, and both people in the interaction become learners and teachers, teaching and learning with each other.

QUESTIONS: Am I open to changing my opinion based on what my conversation partners say? Do I balance telling and asking? Am I confident in myself and in my conversation partners? Do my conversation partners feel safe telling me what they think? Do I really want what is best for my conversation partners?

Reflection

The principle: I engage in conversations that look back, look at, and look ahead.

WHAT IT LOOKS LIKE

Thinking through challenges and opportunities is a truly enjoyable experience. We are wired to be creative and solve problems, and sometimes problem solving or creating can bring some much-needed order to a chaotic situation. When we tackle a problem or explore how to take advantage of an opportunity, we can be filled with a sense of accomplishment. When we look at data from a classroom, for example, we can feel a boost in energy as we interpret and plan what to do about the data. But problems arise when the observer is the person solving and creating. An administrator or coach who does all the thinking for a teacher robs that teacher of the chance to feel accomplishment and energy for themselves.

Michael Bungay Stanier, the author of *The Advice Trap* (2021), explained this in conversation with Jim on his *Coaching Conversations* podcast. "It feels great to be the person whose doling out advice," Michael said, "because it is a high-status action ... If you're always the person to give advice, you're fundamentally saying to the other person, you're not good enough to come up with this answer by yourself. I'm better than you."

When we give advice and thereby take away our conversation partner's opportunity to reflect for themselves, we take away that person's opportunity to clarify the challenge for themselves and to own the solution. As Michael points out in *The Advice Trap*, the research is clear, we think our advice is much more valuable than it is, and we think other people want it much more than they do. Similarly, Nancy Kline writes that we "assume that the best help we can be to people is to do their thinking for them, to give them our ideas, to interrupt them and tell them what to think" (2020, p. 31).

How then do we explore data in a way that encourages others to reflect, problem solve, invent, and create? How do we avoid what Michael Bungay Stanier refers to as "the advice trap"? Our *advice* ☺ is to replace advice giving with asking real questions. Michael has a question that we love to ask: "You've probably thought a lot about this; what are you thinking you might do?" We have found that that simple question almost always leads others to share their thinking about what they might do.

In *The Definitive Guide to Instructional Coaching* (Knight, 2022), Jim wrote about the characteristics of effective questions. A number of the characteristics he identified are included below.

EASY

Good questions are easy to answer. This means the questions are short and the language is clear and precise. Also, good questioners ask one question at a time and then wait for a complete answer before asking another question.

WORTH ANSWERING

Although good questions are easy to answer, they still need to be worth asking. Sometimes people talk about probing questions, but we don't like the term "probing questions" because, as qualitative researcher Irving Seidman has written, the word "conveys a sense of the powerful interview treating the participant as an object" (2013, p. 86). We prefer instead to describe questions as invitational—a good question invites another to go deeper; to consider other perspectives, challenges, or opportunities; or to imagine a new positive vision for the future.

FOCUSED ON THE PERSON ANSWERING, NOT THE PERSON ASKING

Some questions call attention to the person who is asking them rather than the person who is answering. For example, we can ask questions that show off our cleverness, such as a question to which we know the answer but that our conversation partner likely doesn't. But good questions shouldn't show off the questioner's brilliance. They should shine a light on the person answering the question.

POSITIVE

Writers such as Tony Grant (2003) who study solution-focused coaching suggest that questions are more effective when they evoke positive futures rather than identify roadblocks. For example, most people are more motivated by the question "What would it look like if this class was going exactly as you hope?" than the question "What's not going well in your class?" Identifying challenges and roadblocks can be an important part of coaching, but we suggest considering whether a question would be more effective if it was asked more positively.

REAL

Some questions are just advice with a question mark at the end. To ask, "Don't you think your students would get more out of the class if you used more small-group activities?" isn't really a question. Good questions, as journalist Kate Murphy (2019) has written, "don't have a hidden agenda of fixing, saving, advising, or correcting" but rather allow "people to tell their stories, express their realities, and find the resources within themselves to figure out how they feel about a problem and decide on next steps" (p. 147).

COMMUNICATE RESPECT AND BUILD CONNECTIONS

Questions can build or damage connections between people. Good questions invite people to think deeper while also communicating respect, such as is the case with Michael Bungay Stanier's question, "You've probably thought a lot about this, what are you thinking you might do?" Less effective questions communicate moralistic judgment, such as "Don't you think your students would learn more if you stated the outcomes more clearly?" As coaching expert Julie Starr (2016) has written, "Great questions avoid making somebody wrong" (p. 96).

FAVORITE QUESTIONS

We have found it helpful to act on Christian van Nieuwerburgh's suggestion (2017) to write down a list of our favorite questions. Over time, we have identified questions that open up conversations or move them forward. Of course, questions shouldn't be used in a rote way. Coaching should always be a unique conversation based on the conversation partner's concerns. As Christian has written, "Very often ... the most helpful question will emerge from a coachee's response if a coach is listening genuinely" (p. 50).

QUESTION: Can I stay curious and avoid the Advice Trap?

Praxis

The principle: I structure learning so that it is grounded in real life.

Data have enormous potential for accelerating professional learning. Data show us where we are, where we want to get to, and what kind of progress we are making. But data's real power is only realized when data are used in connection with professional learning. Data by themselves, especially negative data, can inhibit professional learning. A teacher who sees that her students aren't learning as she expected but doesn't have any idea how to help her students learn is a teacher who lacks hope.

We suggest that data be used within a model for professional learning that builds hope by helping teachers (a) get a clear picture of reality, (b) set goals, (c) identify pathways to the goal (often teaching strategies), (d) monitor progress, and (e) increase their motivation by revealing when progress is being made. In Chapter 4 we discuss the proposed model for integrating data and professional learning—the Impact Cycle.

QUESTION: Do I share data that are tied to a change process such as the Impact Cycle?

Reciprocity

The principle: I enter each conversation open and expecting to learn.

When we see others as equals, we expect to learn from them. Some might ask, "Do you mean that I should be able to learn from that brand-new teacher with only two months' experience?" Our answer is yes; if we really embrace the Partnership Principles, we should see everyone we meet as a person who teaches us something. The new teacher may not know as much about pedagogy or content as an experienced coach or administrator, but that teacher might see something about students that we don't see.

One way to think about the Partnership Principles is to ask, "If someone was talking with us about data related to our work, how would we like them to interact with us?" Chances are, we'd be more inclined to learn from them if we sensed that they were really interested in what we had to say and if we thought they really wanted to learn from us. Chances are we'd find it easier to talk with someone who didn't act like they thought they were better than us. Chances are we'd be more inclined to learn from someone who saw our strengths and helped us see them, too. Chances are we'd prefer to learn with someone who clearly had our best interests at heart. Chances are we'd want to work with some who asked respectful questions that helped us move forward, who listened to us in a way that showed that they authentically valued our opinions. Chances are we'd be more inclined to learn from someone who treated us like a partner.

QUESTION: Do I enter into every conversation expecting to learn from my conversation partner?

To Sum Up

As discussed in this chapter, conversations about data may fail when the Data Rules are ignored and when observers communicate that somebody isn't (a) good, (b) competent, (c) accepted, or (d) autonomous. If people embrace the Partnership Principles, they likely would adhere to the following:

EQUALITY: Not interrupt, not moralistically judge.

CHOICE: Not try to control.

VOICE: Listen authentically, both internally and externally.

DIALOGUE: Be open to being changed by others' opinions, balance telling with asking, and genuinely keep their conversation partners' best interests at heart. Also, use data as a third point for dialogue.

REFLECTION: Replace their desire to give advice with effective questions.

PRAXIS: Keep data as a part of professional development that provides pathways people can follow to meet their goals.

RECIPROCITY: Go into every data conversation expecting to learn from their conversation partner.

Making It Real

Students

Many of the communication beliefs and skills described in this chapter could be taught to and practiced by students. Since students spend a lot of their time working in groups or teams and learning together, they would benefit from improving their listening and questioning skills, being open to others' opinions, avoiding moralistic judgments, or having the best interests of others at heart. Positive, life-giving communication is more than a way of talking—partnership communication is a life skill anyone can apply to all the conversations they have in life.

Teachers

We encourage educators to consider how they can apply the partnership approach in the classroom. Avoiding moralistic judgment, communicating that we believe in our students, listening, and asking respectful, powerful questions should create learner-friendly environments for students. But other aspects of the partnership approach should also be considered. How can learning be connected with real-life experience? What happens when students have more control over their learning? Do I, as a teacher, expect to learn from my students? Can learning be more dialogical and less directive? Questions like these open up many possibilities for how students learn in school.

Coaches

The partnership approach has been designed especially for coaches who are engaged in learning partnerships with teachers. We found (Knight, 2018) that when coaches work from the Partnership Principles and implement the partnership communication strategies described in this chapter, their coaching has an unmistakably positive impact on teachers and, indeed, on student learning and well-being. The challenge is that often people are unaware of what their communication strategies look like in reality. For this reason, we highly recommend that coaches watch themselves on video to assess whether the way they communicate is in alignment with the Partnership Principles and communication strategies.

Administrators

By the very nature of their position, administrators are faced with the challenge that they have structural power within an organization, and that structural power inter- feres with their ability to communicate from a partnership perspective. Research conducted by Dacher Keltner (2016) shows that when we have structural power, we may lose our capacity for empathy towards those who report to us. For example, when change isn't happening in the way we had hoped, we can slip into blaming those whom we lead (the same thing can happen in the classroom where teachers have structural power over students). Additionally, people who report to those in structurally powerful positions may lose empathy for their leaders. Chances are you've heard teachers talk about administrators in moralistically judgmental ways.

The problems caused by structural power make the partnership approach particularly important. Because people are less inclined to believe that their bosses care about them, and because bosses may be less inclined to care, leaders need to actively demonstrate partnership communication skills like openness, effective listening, respectful questioning, and authentic benevolence for others. As with coaches, administrators can learn a lot by watching videos of their meetings and other interactions with colleagues.

Going Deeper

We developed the Partnership Principles as a result of our readings in many different fields, but two books in particular were especially influential: Paulo Freire's *Pedagogy of the Oppressed* (1970) and Peter Block's *Stewardship* (2013). Freire's work is inspiring, philosophical, and a challenging read, but his ideas about mutually humanizing conversations have influenced a generation of educational theorists. Block's book introduced us to the concept of partnership as a metaphor for interaction. Both books are decades old, but they remain especially relevant today.

The best books on listening we've read are Kate Murphy's *You're Not Listening* (2020) and Nancy Kline's *The Promise That Changes Everything* (2020). Murphy's book is engaging, extremely helpful, and fun to read. Kline's book is beautifully written, poetic, but also filled with practical suggestions about listening, questioning, and the components of thinking environments.

Many books have influenced our thinking on dialogue, including Freire's *Pedagogy of the Oppressed*, mentioned above. Two of the most important books on the study of dialogue are David Bohm's *On Dialogue* (1996) and William Isaacs' *Dialogue* (1999). Bohm's text, which is a short presentation that has been transcribed and turned into a little book, is almost a love letter to better conversations. Bohm shares several important ideas that have shaped a generation of writing about dialogue. Isaacs' book is a comprehensive overview filled with practical strategies and theoretical concepts related to dialogue.

THE IMPACT CYCLE

is about

a structure for making powerful,
positive improvements

begin

*get ready to
implement*

*make adaptations
until the goal is met*

Identify

Learn

Improve

CHAPTER 4

THE IMPACT CYCLE

This chapter explains how to use data to improve teaching, using a universal model for change called the Impact Cycle. It's a simple process with three stages: Identify, Learn, Improve. In the Identify stage, you gather data, set a goal, and figure out what data to gather to measure progress. In the Learn stage, you learn what you need to know to achieve your goal. Finally, in the Improve stage, you make changes until you reach your goal. If you already know the Impact Cycle well, you might skip this chapter; however, even if you are familiar with the Impact Cycle, this chapter will deepen your understanding by making explicit the connection between data and the cycle.

CHAPTER RESOURCES

Access charts, diagrams, research, and resources from this chapter.

What you do makes a difference, and you have to decide what kind of difference you want to make.

JANE GOODALL

Mark Verde is a vice principal of Learning and Curriculum at Bangkok Patana School, a British International School in Thailand. Mark was one of six participants in a research study Jim conducted during the 2022–23 academic year exploring "A Year in the Life of a Coach."[1] During the study, Mark and Jim sent each other messages several times a week on the video chat app Marco Polo (www.marcopolome.com) so Jim could better understand the big and small details of Mark's work as a coach.

Mark loved coaching and he loved students, especially the youngest children he worked with, and each message he sent was inevitably a bright spot in Jim's day. Mark was a valuable resource for Jim because he had at least three perspectives on coaching: Mark experienced (a) being coached as a teacher, (b) coaching other teachers, and (c) guiding Patana's elementary coaching program. Viewing coaching from many perspectives, Mark was convinced that coaching was essential for his school's continuous improvement.

Data were an important part of the coaching that Mark and others did at Patana. Mark video recorded his own lessons and used the interaction analysis tool (described in Chapter 7) to gain insight into how he built connection with students. In addition, he gathered data on behavioral, cognitive, and emotional engagement with many of the teachers he coached. He told Jim he was seeing "massive gains," for example, when he asked students to report on their engagement through the use of exit tickets.

---

[1] Jim presented his findings in 2023 at the Teaching, Learning, Coaching Conference in Orlando, Florida.

One educator Mark partnered with was Pinkarn Vajrapana (Pim), a highly respected leader at Patana, who was head of the Thai program across the school. Pim usually taught secondary students, but in her role as head of the Thai program, she was also required to teach three elementary classes. Pim discovered, as many teachers before her have discovered, that elementary students require different teaching strategies than secondary students.

Committed to excellence, Pim wanted to be a great model for other teachers in the Thai program. She wanted her elementary students to flourish in the way her secondary students were, so in order to move forward, she agreed to partner with Mark for coaching. Mark had participated in online and face-to-face coaching courses offered by Jim, and he chose to use the Impact Cycle (Knight, 2018) as the coaching process with Pim.

The Impact Cycle (Knight, 2018), developed over two decades at the Instructional Coaching Group, is a universal model for change. The cycle is a deceptively simple process anyone can use, on their own or with others, to connect data with professional growth so teachers can make unmistakably positive improvements in student engagement, well-being, or learning. We deliberately emphasize that the cycle is "deceptively" simple, for, in reality, coaches who implement the cycle and embrace the Partnership Principles must learn a nuanced way of communicating. On the one hand, instructional coaches should have deep knowledge of effective instruction and, when appropriate, they need to share that knowledge so that teachers and their students flourish. On the other hand, instructional coaches who take the partnership approach recognize that simply telling teachers what to do, without involving them in the process of solving an issue facing them, increases the likelihood of teacher resistance and inhibits teachers' professional growth.

When coaches take a dialogical approach to guiding change, they (a) say what they think when it is helpful and (b) recognize that people only do what they choose to do. They share their ideas (during goal setting or while explaining strategies, for example), but they recognize the teacher as the decision maker, in part, because the teacher really is the decision maker. Most teachers won't fully embrace a strategy unless they are convinced it is worth the effort.

The dialogical approach is implicit in all three stages of the Impact Cycle: Identify, Learn, Improve. Each of the stages and how they reflect the Partnership Principles are described below.

Identify

___

During the Identify stage of the Impact Cycle, teachers, often in partnership with a coach or administrator, gather data so that they can identify (a) a clear picture of current reality, (b) a goal, and (c) a pathway to the goal (often a teaching strategy).

Using Data to Get a Clear Picture of Reality

People engaged in any kind of improvement activity usually start with a clear picture of reality for at least two reasons. First, and perhaps most obvious, if people do not have a clear picture of reality, they risk investing a lot of energy pursuing the wrong goal. If we want to change some aspect of our reality, we need to know what that reality looks like. Second, a clear picture of reality is essential for motivation. People are motivated when they see a gap between their current reality and their hoped-for future (Miller & Rollnick, 2013). When people do not see reality clearly, they may not feel the need to change.

Data are an essential part of getting a clear picture of reality because, as we like to say, data make the invisible, visible.[2] Teachers who understand how to use single-point rubrics (described in Chapter 6) to gather data on students' writing, for example, will know more about what their students can and cannot do than teachers who don't know how to gather those data. Similarly, teachers who understand students' emotional engagement in school (or lack of engagement) will better understand what they need to do to create conditions that help students see that they belong in school. When teachers have a clear understanding of student achievement

---

[2]We're not certain who first coined this phrase, but we saw it first in *Got Data? Now What?* (2012) by Laura Lipton and Bruce Wellman.

and engagement, they write better goals, and when those goals are met, students experience better learning and well-being.

There are many ways in which teachers can get a clear picture of reality either with a coach or on their own. We will highlight four.

1. RECORD THE LESSON. As we mentioned in Chapter 1, video is a powerful way for teachers to get a clear picture of reality. When people review video of themselves doing their work, they move from talking about change to doing something about change. Video cuts through our defense mechanisms and perceptual errors, and it empowers us to see reality as it really is.

When coaches collaborate with teachers on a coaching cycle, they often video record collaborating teachers' lessons and share the video with the teachers. Then, teachers can review video of their lesson before meeting with their coach to set goals. We have found that it is best for coach and teacher to watch the video separately first and then discuss it during a goal-setting meeting.

Video can be recorded in different ways to support teachers depending on what they prefer. For example, a coach recording a lesson can turn the camera toward the teacher when the teacher is instructing and turn the camera toward students when they are engaged in group activities or classroom discussion. For a variety of reasons, some teachers prefer that the camera only focuses on students. A teacher interested in the impact of her questioning, for example, may want to keep the camera focused on students for the entire lesson so that she can assess the impact of various kinds of questions.

Other teachers may prefer that the lesson be audio recorded. One advantage of this approach is that a teacher can listen to the lesson on their phone as they drive home from school. But while audio is a lot more helpful than nothing, compared to video, it doesn't reflect the same level of data; for example, nonverbal communication is lost if a class is only audio recorded.

We have found that teachers get more out of watching video if they keep an observation form nearby to focus their observations while they watch the recorded lesson.

We suggest two forms, included below, but of course, you may use whatever form you find most useful. The kinds of data listed on the forms are described in detail in Chapters 5, 6, and 7.

WATCH YOUR STUDENTS

Date:

After watching the video of today's class, please answer the following questions to assess how close your students' behavior was to your goal for an ideal class.

How many students were in the class for the video-recorded lesson?

What percentage of the students appeared to be behaviorally engaged?

What percentage of the students appeared to be cognitively engaged?

How many questions did you ask?

How many different students answered questions?

How many students gave correct answers to questions?

How many students did not answer any questions?

What percentage of the lesson was non-productive time?

What percentage of the lesson was productive time?

How many different student disruptions did you see during the recording?

How many comments did students make during the lesson?

How many of the students' responses were high level?

In your opinion, how many students appeared to be learning?

In your opinion, how many students appeared to be interested in the lesson?

What else did you notice as you watched your lesson?

WATCH YOURSELF

Date:

After watching the video of today's class, please answer the following questions to assess how close your students' behavior was to your goal for an ideal class.

Teacher and Student Talk
How many minutes did you talk?
How many minutes did your students talk?
How many minutes were you and your students unintentionally talking at the same time?

Ratio of Interaction
How many times did you direct your attention to students who were acting appropriately?
How many times did you direct your attention to students who were acting inappropriately?

Questions
How many questions did you ask?
What type of questions did you ask?

Open Questions	Closed Questions

Opinion Questions	Right-or-Wrong Questions

Knowledge Questions	Skill Questions	Big Idea Questions

Watch Yourself form continues on next page.

Self-Assessment of the Lesson

After watching the video of today's class, please rate how close your instruction was to your ideal in the following areas.

I clearly explained expectations prior to each activity.

| 1 | 2 | 3 | 4 | 5 | 6 | 7 | 8 | 9 | 10 |

My corrections were calm, consistent, immediate, and planned in advance.

| 1 | 2 | 3 | 4 | 5 | 6 | 7 | 8 | 9 | 10 |

My questions were at the appropriate level (Know, Understand, Do).

| 1 | 2 | 3 | 4 | 5 | 6 | 7 | 8 | 9 | 10 |

My learning structures (stories, cooperative learning, thinking devices, experiential learning) were effective.

| 1 | 2 | 3 | 4 | 5 | 6 | 7 | 8 | 9 | 10 |

I used a variety of learning structures effectively.

| 1 | 2 | 3 | 4 | 5 | 6 | 7 | 8 | 9 | 10 |

I clearly understand what my students know and don't know.

| 1 | 2 | 3 | 4 | 5 | 6 | 7 | 8 | 9 | 10 |

What else did you notice about the lesson?

2. GIVE STUDENTS VOICE. Students are a great untapped source of helpful data when it comes to professional learning in schools. In 2019 there were more than 600 million students in secondary schools around the world (statistica.com), and even though those students could provide valuable information about their experiences in school, most of them rarely, if ever, were asked to share their perspective on their classes.

Asking students to share their thoughts about their learning experiences also increases their engagement. As student-voice expert Russ Quaglia told Jim in a podcast interview posted October 17, 2023, students who say they have a voice are three times more likely to have greater self-worth, five times more likely to be engaged in learning, and five times more likely to have a sense of purpose than students who say they don't have a voice in school (Knight [Host] October 17, 2023, Russ Quaglia, *Coaching Conversations* [Audio Podcast]).

PODCAST: STUDENT VOICE

Listen to Russ and Jim's conversation about student voice on the *Coaching Conversations* podcast.

One way to give students a voice in class is to ask them for feedback on their classroom experiences. For example, teachers may ask students to answer simple questions about learning in class on exit tickets they complete before they leave class. Teachers may also ask students for suggestions on how the class might be improved. Although student feedback might not provide perfectly reliable data since people often bias high or low for a variety of reasons when they self-report, even imperfect student data can provide helpful information on what could be changed to improve students' learning experiences.

Student interviews are another way to gain valuable data. Interviews can be conducted by a coach who interviews students in the hall or outside class at lunch time, for example, or by the teacher during class when students are engaged in a learning activity that doesn't need constant teacher supervision (coaches could interview students at that time as well). Student interviews are especially helpful when teachers aren't sure why students are acting a certain way during class.

When deciding to conduct interviews, care needs to be taken to select students who will give the most useful information in a given situation. Consider interviewing a range of students—students who are thriving or struggling, students who are neurodiverse, students who act in introverted or extroverted ways, students who are active bilingual learners of English (ABLE; Przymus, et al., 2022), and students who are fluent first-language speakers. When choosing which students to interview, educators should be guided by an overarching question: "Who will help me learn the most about how to make this the best class for all students?"

Interview questions should be tailored to each unique classroom, but some questions, included below, have proven to be especially helpful. Whoever does the interview should listen authentically and nonjudgmentally. If a teacher or coach reacts defensively to negative student feedback, students will be less likely to share their thoughts candidly. No matter what students say, the interviewer should always thank students for their feedback. The interviewer should also keep notes watching for themes.

Over time, an interviewer might stop asking some questions if they keep getting the same answer. Instead the interviewer can start to go deeper into other themes that are coming through in the interviews. The teacher or coach who does the interviews is like an anthropologist trying to see the class through students' eyes to find information they can use to improve the class for students. When a particular comment shows up in many interviews, it is likely a sign that it is a theme that needs to be addressed through an Impact Cycle.

POSSIBLE QUESTIONS FOR STUDENT INTERVIEWS

1. What do you want your teacher to know about you?
2. What was one of the best days in class?
3. What was one of the worst days in class?
4. What is a moment in class that sums up how you feel about this class?
5. How would you describe the class: Is it too easy? Too difficult? Just right?
6. What are one or two things your teacher could do today to make this a better class for you and everyone?
7. What do your friends say about this class?

Finally, teachers can learn from students through classroom discussions about students' learning experiences. To have this kind of conversation with their students, teachers must create psychologically safe environments for conversation. Teachers can create a safe environment by validating every student comment. Every student response should be validated by the teacher and include thanking students for their comments, no matter how positive or negative. Teachers can even respond to comments that might seem silly at first, such as "I think we should be paid to come to school," in ways that uncover the potentially useful aspects of what students say by countering: "What kind of rewards really matter to you when it comes to learning?"

Facilitating a discussion is always a delicate dance since people, young and old, often express more negative than positive comments in groups. Teachers can moderate student comments, ensuring a balance of perspectives while also ensuring that students feel that their comments are welcome. Sometimes teachers need to take a critical, negative comment, such as "I don't think any adults care about us in this school," and turn it into a constructive comment, such as "What would it look and feel like if you felt the adults here really did care?" or "What are some simple things adults could do to show you that they care?" Often this kind of discussion can be handled well by a coach. Besides, students may sometimes be more forthcoming with a coach than a teacher because they interact daily with teachers and are graded by teachers.

3. REVIEW STUDENT WORK. In Chapter 6 we suggest many kinds of data educators can gather to better understand how well their students are learning, including quizzes, tests, questions, checks for understanding, single-point rubrics, and analytical rubrics. Each of these ways of assessing achievement can be used on their own or in combination. For example, a test can be given at the start of a unit to pre-assess student learning, which can help with planning instruction and setting goals.

Sometimes educators choose to assess student performance informally. A coach might ask a teacher, "What do you want your students to be able to do that you don't see them doing now?" A question like that can help teachers identify where they want their students to go and how they'll measure student progress. We don't believe a "pretest" is always essential. In education, as in life, we must often choose what's most practical, and if a teacher creates a single-point rubric, for example, she doesn't need to do a special assignment separate from instruction. Once she uses the rubric, she'll see how well her students are performing.

Some contend that educators only need to assess student learning. If students are learning, they suggest, that's all that matters. However, if educators focus exclusively on achievement, they won't see how much instructional time is unproductive, the percentage of time students vs. teachers talk during a lesson, the percentage of students on task, the number of different students answering questions, and so forth. One approach is to consider both engagement and achievement data to get a more well-rounded understanding of what happens during a lesson. Whatever data are gathered, what matters most is that the data provide a point of departure so that meaningful improvements can be put in place to increase students' learning and well-being.

4. CONDUCT CLASSROOM OBSERVATIONS. One final method of data gathering is having an observer, a coach or administrator, sit in a teacher's classroom and gather various kinds of data on a specially designed form. The 20-Minute High-Impact Survey form included below, discussed in more detail in Chapter 8, includes many types of data described in this book. Most teacher evaluation involves observation of this sort followed by a conversation about the data.

There are some advantages to an observer gathering data in the classroom for teachers. The process is efficient. As the title suggests, the survey we've included takes 20 minutes to complete, and teachers don't need to watch video. Also, getting a comprehensive overview of the classroom is helpful and, in some cases, also necessary, such as for teacher evaluation. However, the problem with this kind of data gathering is that most people don't view reality accurately because their defense mechanisms and perceptual errors get in the way. Most of us see our reality differently than it really is, and consequently we find it difficult to accept others' descriptions of what we do.

In situations where a comprehensive assessment of the classroom is required, we suggest educators use a form like the one included here to evaluate their lessons. When observation is used for teacher evaluation, we suggest that a lesson be video recorded by an administrator and that the teacher and administrator subsequently watch the lesson separately. After watching the video, the teachers and administrator can get together to compare their thoughts about the lesson. When administrators and teachers use video as a third point for dialogue, their conversations are usually more productive than if there is no video (Knight, 2014).

Video was an important way of gathering data when Mark and Pim collaborated. Mark suggested to Pim that they kick off the coaching process by video recording her class to get a clear picture of reality. After getting Pim's agreement, Mark video

20-MINUTE HIGH-IMPACT SURVEY

Community Building

Time on Task

MINUTES	STUDENTS	ON TASK	% ON TASK
:10			
:20			

Ratio of Interactions

REINFORCING	CORRECTING

Disruptions

Teacher / Student Talk

Instructional Time

Check which of the following teaching practices were present and record the number of minutes for each:

CHECK	PRACTICE/ACTIVITY	MINUTES	CHECK	PRACTICE/ACTIVITY	MINUTES
	Beginning routine			Transition time	
	Stories			Quizzes	
	Thinking prompts				
	Cooperative learning				
	Experiential learning				
	Labs				
	Seat work				
	Direct instruction				

Kinds of Questions

OPEN	CLOSED

Levels of Questions

KNOWLEDGE	SKILL	BIG IDEA

Planning, Assessment, Learning

	YES	NO
Teacher clearly states learning target for the lesson.		
Teacher clearly describes success criteria for student learning.		
Teacher gathers data showing whether or not students are learning.		
Teacher modifies teaching or learning to improve student achievement based on data gathered.		

recorded a lesson and sent clips of the lesson to Pim so she could watch them on her own. When he watched the video, Mark noticed that behavioral engagement (described in Chapter 5) was an issue. Pim believed in the students, and she wanted them to succeed, but frequently the students didn't listen to her. They were off task a lot of the time and they often didn't answer Pim's questions. When Mark and Pim first talked, Pim had expressed an interest in improving student learning. Mark wondered if she'd be interested in the same goal when she met with him to talk about the video and set a goal for coaching.

PEERS Goals

After teachers get a clear picture of reality, their attention turns to identifying the goal they want to meet. Once Pim had watched the video, she met with Mark to discuss her perspective on the class and to identify the goal she wanted to set for coaching. In many schools, teachers bring focus to the change they want to see by setting SMART goals (Specific, Measurable, Actionable, Relevant, Timely[3]). SMART goals have a compelling acronym (who doesn't want to be smart?), and they guide people to think deeply and precisely about the goals they set. When people are specific about their goals and make them measurable, their goals are usually more effective than vague statements about preferred futures (see Grant Halvorson, 2012, for an accessible summary of the research on goal setting). However, SMART goals leave out some important aspects of goal setting.

One challenging aspect of SMART goals is the idea that they should be timely. Setting a timely goal is helpful when there is only one person involved in hitting the goal. A person can confidently set the goal of cleaning their basement by Sunday night, for example, if they're the only one doing the cleaning. However, timely goals are less helpful when several people are involved. As a result, setting a time limit for a goal for students who all learn in their own unique ways at their own unique pace seems at best a wild guess.

---

[3]The concept of SMART goals is often attributed to George T. Doran, who introduced this framework in a paper titled "There's a S.M.A.R.T. way to write management's goals and objectives" (1981). Over the years, there have been many different variations on what SMART actually means.

We have found that SMART goals also miss other aspects of effective goal setting in classrooms. For example, SMART goals do not emphasize the importance of setting emotionally compelling goals. We are less likely to hit a goal if we're not that committed to it. The SMART goal framework also overlooks the importance of reducing friction when trying to hit goals. The more difficult a goal is to hit, the less likely it will be hit. Finally, and perhaps most important, the SMART goals framework does not address one of the main things we've learned: Goals need to be student-focused not teacher-focused. As an alternative to SMART goals, we suggest PEERS goals (we've got our own acronym, too!).

PEERS GOALS

POWERFUL

EASY

EMOTIONALLY COMPELLING

REACHABLE (a clear finish line and an identified strategy)

STUDENT-FOCUSED

PEERS goals are powerful. When PEERS goals are met, there are lasting, socially significant improvements in students' lives. PEERS goals are also relatively easy to accomplish. But since PEERS goals are set for powerful changes in the classroom, educators are sure to face productive struggle. Anyone trying to have an unmistakably positive impact on students will experience productive struggle. The best possible goals are extremely powerful and relatively easy to hit. When it comes to deep change, easy and powerful are the way to go.

PEERS goals are also emotionally compelling. Most of us won't want to do the hard work of hitting a goal we are only lukewarm about. Teachers should set goals that address issues they think about when they drive home from school or that wake them up in the middle of the night. As Jim Collins and Jerry Porras have written, a powerful goal "engages people—it reaches out and grabs them in the gut. It is tangible, energizing, highly focused. People 'get it' right away; it takes little or no explanation" (1994, p. 94).

PEERS goals are reachable, which is to say they foster hope (Lopez, 2014). As we mentioned in Chapter 2, hope involves a goal (something to hope for), a strategy (a way to hit the goal), and agency (a belief that we can hit the goals). Reachable goals have two of these attributes. First, reachable goals involve measurable, clearly defined outcomes. Reachable goals don't have to be measured numerically, although that is often the case; but they need to have a very clear finish line. Additionally, reachable goals have an identified strategy that can be used by a teacher to attempt to hit the goal.

Finally, PEERS goals are student- rather than teacher-focused. A teacher-focused goal might be that I am going ask more open-ended questions. A student-focused goal would be that I want 90% engagement during classroom discussion. Student-focused goals put everyone's attention where it needs to be, on students. At the same time, student-focused goals provide a built-in standard for excellent implementation of a strategy. To hit student-focused goals, teachers need to keep refining their practice until it makes the difference it is intended to make.

About his use of the Impact Cycle, Mark told Jim, "I think the biggest lesson we learned was to focus on the students and not the strategies around the playbook. I think the biggest lesson was that we have to say, 'Let's look at the children first. Look at your video, look at your classroom.' Once we know what they need, then we'll look at the strategy."

Coaches who take a dialogical approach to helping teachers set measurable goals ask questions that invite teachers to think deeply about current reality and potential goals. Over the years, Jim and his colleagues have identified several questions that coaches have found to be effective for talking about what data to gather for goal setting.

Every coaching conversation will be different, but coaches often begin with questions that guide teachers to reflect on current reality. Coaches might ask, for example, "On a scale of 1–10, how close was that lesson to a 10?" After the teacher answers, a coach could ask, "Sounds like you've already accomplished a lot. How did you get to that number?" or, "Why did you pick that number?"

After the teacher has talked about current reality, the coach can guide them to talk about a change they'd like to see in the future by asking, for example, "What could you do to move closer to a 10?" The coach can bring focus to the conversation by asking, "Do you want that to be your goal?" and, "If that was your goal, would it really matter to you?" If the teacher responds yes—that goal would matter—the coach and teacher can move on to discussing how to measure the goal. If the teacher doesn't consider the goal to be emotionally compelling, the coach and teacher can explore other options until an emotionally compelling goal has been set.

Most coaches have to learn to let teachers set their own goals during this stage. We like to solve problems (for ourselves and others), and most of us struggle with the temptation to tell others how to fix their problem. We have found, however, for all the reasons mentioned in Chapter 2, that a less than perfect goal chosen by the teacher is better than the perfect goal chosen by the coach (Stoltzfus, 2005). This does not mean that a coach should sit silently if a teacher seems to be setting a goal that is missing an important issue in the classroom. In such a situation, the coach can ask, "Do you mind if I share something I'm wondering about?" and then tell the teacher the concern. A coach might say, for example, "I noticed that the same four students answered all the questions you asked. The video showed 18 students did not answer any questions during the discussion. Is that something you want to address?" By proposing a suggestion as a question rather than a directive, the coach increases the likelihood the teacher will embrace the suggestion.

THE IDENTIFY QUESTIONS FOR EXPLORING REALITY AND SETTING GOALS

On a scale of 1–10, how close was that class to your ideal class?

Why did you pick that number?

What would have to change to move it closer to a 10?

What would you like your students to do that they aren't doing now?

Do you want that to be your goal?

If that was your goal, would you really care about the goal?

When Mark met with Pim to set a PEERS goal, he used many of the Identify questions to ask Pim about how she saw her students performing and what she wanted them to do that they weren't doing. Mark was impressed by Pim's willingness to confront reality. Mark told Jim, "She's got a very, very big position in the school, and yet she was willing to be vulnerable in that role." Pim could see she needed to change how learning was happening if her class was going to reach a 10 on her scale.

Before watching her video, Pim had wanted to work on academics, but after she watched video of her class, Mark said, "the penny dropped." Like Mark, Pim noticed that students weren't on task, weren't listening, and weren't answering questions. With Mark asking Pim questions that invited her to think deeply about how students were experiencing her class, she was able to quickly identify her goals: "I want the children to listen. I want them to sit still. I want them to show that they're learning." After Pim was clear on her goal, Mark and Pim turned to identifying the data Pim would gather to measure progress toward her goal.

Identifying How to Measure the Goal

Coaches can also take a dialogical approach to identifying how the goal will be measured and what data will be gathered to measure progress toward the goal. Sometimes teachers know what kind of data they want to gather, or they know what it will look like if they hit their goal, so coaches don't need to make any suggestions. Such was the case with Pim, who had a clear picture in mind of what her students would look like if they were listening, answering questions, and showing that they were learning.

But in other situations, the coach and teacher will want to make their goal precise by identifying measurable outcomes. In such conversations, the coach might ask, "What will be different for students if we hit this goal?" and, "What kind or kinds of data should we gather to measure that change in your students?" If the teacher has some solid suggestions for what kind of data to collect, the coach doesn't need to add anything. But if the teacher is uncertain about how to measure change, the coach, after asking for permission to share, might say something like, "Other teachers I've worked with who set behavioral engagement goals usually set goals around time on task, reducing the number of disruptions, decreasing wasted time, or changing the way students respond to questions. Which of those kinds of data would best tell you whether or not you are moving toward your goal?"

Identifying Strategies to Hit the Goal

During the last step of the Identify stage, teachers identify the strategy they will use to try to hit their goal. To provide the most effective support for this step, coaches need to have a deep knowledge of effective teaching practices. Coaches can develop their expertise by creating instructional playbooks (Knight et al., 2020). These are documents, in print or digital format, that consist of three parts: (a) a list of the highest-impact strategies teachers use in the school or district, (b) one-page documents summarizing the most important information about those strategies, and (c) checklists that coaches can use to explain the strategies clearly so teachers can implement them easily.

When coaches take a dialogical approach and partner with teachers to identify a strategy the teacher will use to try to hit the goal, they ensure that the teachers continue to be the decision makers during coaching. Coaches learn to let go of the temptation to tell teachers what to do. At the same time, when necessary, coaches shouldn't stay silent when they can share strategies that might help a teacher hit her goal. They just need to share those strategies dialogically.

How much coaches share during dialogical coaching depends on how much teachers have learned about teaching strategies. We suggest coaches start by asking teachers about their ideas. The coach can suggest they make a list of strategies the teacher might try and then ask questions that help teachers think and talk about how to hit their goal. A coach might say, for example, "You've probably thought a lot about this. What are you thinking you might do to hit your goal?" and then ask, "And what else?" Other questions might include "How have you dealt with this situation in the past?" or "What advice would you give someone else in your situation?" Each time a question elicits a possible strategy, the coach can note it down on the list.

In many cases, teachers are experienced and familiar with teaching practices that they're learned through the years, and they know what they want to try in an attempt to hit their PEERS goal. "What I want to do," they might say, "is ask better questions, more open questions and higher-level questions. I think that's my first step in trying to improve the quality of classroom discussion." If teachers have a good plan and know what they want to do, a coach who offers other suggestions might get in the way.

However, when teachers are stuck or don't know what to do, the coach can help by sharing some suggestions dialogically. For example, the coach might start, as we've discussed previously, by asking for permission to share ideas, saying, "Do you mind if I share some things I've seen other teachers do who were trying to hit behavioral goals like yours?" Then, assuming the teacher says yes, the coach can share suggestions.

A coach, working with a teacher who wants to increase time on task, for example, might say to the teacher, "Well, teachers I've worked with have tried many different strategies. Some teachers try to get really clear on their expectations for activities and transitions and then clearly teach those expectations to students. Other teachers have increased the amount of attention they give students when they are engaged to encourage students to stay on task. Yet other teachers have practiced being really consistent with their corrections. Sometimes teachers try to do all three—expectations, positive attention, and effective corrections. What questions do you have about any of these suggestions?"

After the coach has adequately explained all of the suggested options and added them to the list, they should read through the strategies with the teacher, taking care to not push the teacher toward one particular strategy. If the teacher is going to own the solution, she has to choose the solution. No matter which strategy is chosen, chances are it will have to be adapted and modified. That is why the goal is so important. The effectiveness of the strategy will be determined by whether or not the goal is hit.

QUESTIONS TO IDENTIFY A TEACHING STRATEGY

You've probably thought a lot about this. What are some strategies you might use?

When you've encountered situations like this previously, what has worked for you?

What advice would you give someone else in your situation?

Would you like me to suggest some strategies?

Now that we've listed several possible strategies, which one gives you the most confidence or energy?

At Bangkok Patana School, Mark and his colleagues have adopted Tom Sherrington and Oliver Cavigliolis' *Teaching WalkThrus* (2020) as their instructional playbook. *Teaching WalkThrus* contains 50 high-impact teaching strategies, described through clear explanations and simple but powerful visual illustrations. When Pim and Mark discussed what teaching strategies Pim would use to hit her goal, they turned to *Teaching WalkThrus* and identified three strategies she would use to try and hit the goal: (a) establish your expectations, (b) think, pair, share, and (c) cold calling.

Pim was familiar with *Teaching WalkThrus* as Patana's instructional playbook, so she quickly identified what she would use. Other teachers might reference other teaching strategies, or they might have in mind a particular strategy they want to use to hit their goal. Coaches and teachers might also co-create a list of strategies from which the teacher chooses a strategy. Regardless of how it happens, the people who know the students best and who know how they teach the best should be the people deciding what happens in the classroom.

Learn

During the Learn stage of the Impact Cycle, coaches ensure that teachers are ready to implement the strategies they've identified. To prepare teachers, coaches usually explain strategies with checklists and model strategies in a variety of ways.

Explaining Strategies Using Checklists

Effective instructional coaches explain strategies precisely but provisionally, leaving room for teachers to adapt the strategies based on what they know about their students' needs and their own strengths as teachers. Often coaches use checklists to describe strategies to make it easier for teachers to implement new ways of teaching. We have found that it is most effective for coaches to take a dialogical approach when they describe strategies.

Dialogical explanations are a particularly complex form of communication. On the one hand, the coach's description has to be very clear, otherwise the teacher won't be able to implement the strategy. On the other hand, the coach has to describe the strategy in a way that leaves room for the teacher to adapt it to their students' needs and their own strengths. Teachers need to be able to make the strategy their own.

We suggest coaches explain strategies using a checklist. For example, a coach who is collaborating with a teacher who wants to implement the "I do it, we do it, you do it" teaching routine might share a checklist like the one included below. The coach taking a dialogical approach might share the checklist with the teacher and ask the teacher to look it over to see if they have any questions. After answering the teacher's questions, the coach can go through each item on the checklist, confirming that the teacher understands the explanation and then ask the teacher if they want to make any changes. Often teachers make suggestions that improve how the strategy will be taught or at least make the strategy more effective for a particular group of students. In those cases, the coach adds the teachers' suggested changes on the checklist. At other times, teachers make suggestions that the coach has some concerns about. In those cases, we suggest the conversation might sound something like this:

> Teacher: "I'm thinking I might just skip the 'I do it' phase and dive right into the 'you do it' and get the kids acting right away. I think the 'I do it' might be too boring."

> Coach: "Do you mind if I share some thoughts I have about those changes?"

> Teacher: "Go ahead."

> Coach: "Now, you know your students better than I do, so be sure to do what you think is best, but researchers would likely say that students need to see the practice done well first so they know what to do when they practice. If students don't see the practice done correctly, they

might develop some bad habits. What do you think about that? Those researchers don't know your students or you, so we should do what you think is best."

Teacher: "Well that makes sense, but I still don't want the students to be bored during the 'I do it' part. My modeling won't make much difference if students aren't listening. I'm also not that confident that I can model this strategy very effectively."

Coach: "Well, let's talk about how we can make the 'I do it' more engaging and also how we can make sure you are really confident when doing it."

The dialogical approach is a humble approach. The coach doesn't try to impose their solution onto the teacher. The coach engages the teacher as a partner, a co-thinker. We believe that given the complexity of the classroom, a humble approach is the most realistic and effective approach. Ultimately, most teaching strategies need to be modified to meet the complex demands of the classroom. The true test of how effectively a strategy is taught is whether or not the strategy helps students hit the coaching goal.

 ## I DO IT, WE DO IT, YOU DO IT

I do it	✓
Review prior learning	
Explain why today's learning is important	
Tell students what they need to do	
Think out loud	
Problem solve	
Attack the challenge in different ways	

(Continued)

I do it	
Address categories of error that arose in the previous day's work	

We do it	☑
Ask the students how to do what is being learned	
Call on a variety of students and ask them to explain how to do the task being learned	
Ask students to explain their thinking	
Shape students' responses (connect and redirect)	
Encourage students with praise for effort	
Assess student understanding (perhaps with a quick assessment like response cards)	
Reteach if necessary	

You do it	☑
Let students perform independently	
Give brief constructive feedback	
Give feedback on the fly	
Identify categories of error if students haven't mastered the learning	
Plan how to address the categories of error in the next lesson	
Attack the challenge in different ways	
Address categories of error that arose in the previous day's work	

Modeling

Coaches also often help teachers get ready to try out a new strategy by providing opportunities for teachers to see the strategies in use. Sometimes this means the coach models the strategy in the teacher's classroom with their students. Coaches can also model a strategy without students in the classroom, co-teach, provide an opportunity for the teacher to watch another teacher using the strategy, share a video of someone implementing the strategy, or some combination of these approaches. Whatever form of modeling is used, at the end of the Learn stage of the Impact Cycle, the teacher should feel well prepared to implement the new strategy.

When Mark partnered with Pim so she would be prepared to implement the strategies from *Teaching WalkThrus*, he and Pim looked through the visuals included in WalkThrus in the same way a coach might use a checklist. Sherrington and Cavigliolis' book provides simple five-step descriptions and illustrations of strategies that can be used in the way instructional coaches might use checklists. Pim didn't feel she needed to watch someone model the lessons for her, but she video recorded herself teaching and compared what she saw herself doing in the videos with the descriptions in *Teaching WalkThrus*. In a way, she used video to model implementation for herself.

Improve

____

It would be wonderful if teachers and students always hit their goals right after teachers implemented new strategies. Unfortunately, this usually isn't what happens. Teachers frequently need to make adaptations to hit their goals. There are only a finite number of modifications that can be made by a teacher, and some or all may be made during the Improve stage. Those modifications include (a) changing the strategy, (b) changing how the strategy is taught, (c) changing the goal, (d) changing what data are gathered to show progress toward the goal, and (e) changing nothing and simply waiting until the goal is met.

Data play a central role throughout the Improve stage. As we explain in Chapters 5 and 6, teachers and coaches can gather data on students' progress toward a goal and on the teacher's implementation of a new strategy, and both kinds of data can be used to make adaptations until the goal is met. For example, a teacher who wants to increase engagement during classroom discussion by asking more open questions could review data on student engagement, the questions asked, and the impact of the different types of questions.

Pim made many adaptations along the way, often on her own and sometimes in partnership with Mark. For example, to clarify expectations about where students would sit and with whom by using The Walkthru "Seating Plans," Pim created optimal groupings of students and then labeled where students should sit when they entered the classroom. During "think, pair, share" she practiced making sure she gave students sufficient time to think and then talk. She also ensured that all students were paired with someone they could learn with and not just talk with. "I don't mind the chatter," Pim said, "but it has to be learning chatter."

When Mark talked about his conversations with Pim, he reported that her entire demeanor changed during coaching. Mark said, "You knew she wanted to do the best job possible, but at the start, you could see her uncertainty about it. But by the end of it, she said, 'I know I can do it now.'" More important, Mark said, "This time around, when I coached her, success came so quickly and you could see her [confidence]. She knew she could do it with these children because she knew what strategies to put in place, what steps to take at the start of the year."

For Mark, it was very rewarding "to go in there and see those children responding so positively to their learning and their teacher. And, you know, I went into an environment where I don't understand it. It's all in Thai for me. But I could see it, you know. I could see learning in a different language." In addition, Mark saw Pim's influence on her colleagues. When they saw her success, they wanted to have the same success with their students.

 ## To Sum Up

Data aren't very helpful until they become part of a process for improvement. In this chapter, we proposed the Impact Cycle, which involves three stages: Identify, Learn, Improve. During the Identify stage, data are gathered through reviewing video, giving students voice, reviewing student work, or observing lessons. Data provide a starting point for identifying a goal and a strategy the teacher will use to hit the goal. During the Learn stage, teachers learn what they need to learn to be prepared to implement the strategy they will use to try to hit their goals. During the Improve stage, teachers make adaptations to strategies and goals until the goal is hit.

Making It Real

Students

Students can really help when teachers are implementing the Impact Cycle. Students can share their insights into how a class is progressing, through comments on exit tickets, responses during interviews, or classroom discussions. Additionally, many educators around the world are experimenting with students coaching each other using a change model like the Impact Cycle.[4]

Teachers

Teachers can use the Impact Cycle on their own to make improvements in student learning. They do this by using video or some other method to get a clear picture of reality. Then, they identify their goal and the strategy they will implement to hit the goal. Finally, they continue to gather data and make adaptations until the goal is met. Teachers can also engage in peer coaching activities.[5]

Coaches

When coaches partner with teachers to implement the Impact Cycle, they can make it much easier for teachers to move through the cycle. For example, coaches can help gather data by video recording lessons, interviewing students, facilitating classroom discussions, gathering data on student achievement, or observing classrooms with

---

[4]Growth Coaching International describes one model of students coaching students at this link: https://www.growthcoaching.com.au/courses/students-coaching-students/

[5]Consultants at the Instructional Coaching Group (https://www.instructionalcoaching.com) and GROWTH Coaching International (https://www.growthcoaching.com.au) offer workshops that guide teachers through a PEER coaching process centered on the Impact Cycle.

the 20-minute survey or some other observation form. Coaches can also ask powerful questions that help teachers identify goals and strategies. Because they are experts in effective teaching practices, often instructional coaches help teachers identify and implement practices. Finally, coaches can use powerful questions to help teachers identify adaptations they need to make to strategies in order to meet identified goals.

Administrators

Most administrators already have so many tasks to complete that they will not be able to partner with more than one or two teachers to complete an Impact Cycle. However, they can use aspects of the Impact Cycle as a part of the professional development they conduct with teachers. For example, they can video record teachers' lessons, share the video with teachers, and then ask them to review the video with whatever evaluation tool is used in a district. We feel the use of video should always be a choice. If an administrator is going to use this method, she needs to ensure that she and the teacher have a shared understanding of the observation form.

Administrators can also use the Identify questions or other powerful questions to help teachers identify goals they want to hit and strategies teachers can implement to hit those goals.

Going Deeper

The most extensive description of the Impact Cycle is contained in Jim's book *The Impact Cycle* (Knight, 2018), and anyone interested in getting a deep understanding of the cycle will likely benefit from reading the book. Jim's book *Focus on Teaching* (Knight, 2014) also contains a lot of strategies and tools for use of video as a part of professional learning.

Atul Gawande's book *The Checklist Manifesto* (2009) remains the classic explanation of the power of checklists and clear explanations. Finally, *The Practice of Adaptive Leadership* by Ronald Heifetz, Alexander Grashow, and Marty Linsky (2009) is the go-to book on how to make adaptations during change initiatives.

⊸⊙⊙⊸ PART TWO

KINDS OF DATA

ENGAGEMENT

is about

increasing student learning
and well-being by assessing

*how
students act*

*what students
are learning*

*whether students
feel they belong*

Behavioral
Engagement

Cognitive
Engagement

Emotional
Engagement

CHAPTER 5

ENGAGEMENT

Engagement is an important part of life and learning and should be the concern of everyone in school. In this chapter, we define three categories of engagement—behavioral, cognitive, and emotional—and describe how to gather different kinds of data within those categories. You can skip this chapter if you aren't interested in student engagement, but having said that, we think everyone should be concerned about engagement.

CHAPTER RESOURCES

Access charts, diagrams, research, and resources from this chapter.

To pay attention, this is our endless and proper work.

MARY OLIVER

Kristin Crouch is an instructional coach at Van Rensselaer Elementary in Rensselaer, New York. Like Mark Verde mentioned in Chapter 4, Kristin was one of six participants in Jim's "Year in the Life of a Coach" study (Knight, 2023). Kristin loves learning and consequently loves coaching, and her many messages about the impact she was having inspired Jim as he continued to study the details of coaching. One of her stories was about Carli Imreh-Allegretta.

Carli was teaching 2nd grade temporarily for a teacher who was away on long-term leave. "Like so many teachers," Kristin said, "Carli had a bit of imposter syndrome," which was intensified for Carli because she had such high expectations for her students. She came to Kristin because she wanted her students to do more. Kristin was happy to work with her. She could see that Carli was a very good teacher even though she didn't have a lot of experience teaching. "I had to keep telling her that she was doing so much right," Kristin said.

Kristin video recorded Carli's class, and they first watched the video separately. Both coach and teacher could see that engagement was a problem during center time, where Kristin calculated that time on task was 58%. Frustrated because she knew the class wasn't where it needed to be, Carli set a goal that students would get to 85% time on task, on average, during center time.

"Carli," Kristin said, "was doing a lot of things right." She had a timer to keep track of time, and she listed on the board what students needed to do. Nevertheless, as typical 2nd graders, her students got distracted and off task. Carli wanted to help her students create the habits that would keep them on track, so her first strategy was to check in with students. Kristin said, "Carli would walk around the room, get close to every student, and kind of just do like a check-in." That first strategy moved time on task to 64%.

Then, although all of the tasks were listed on the board already, Carli got more explicit about the tasks students were to perform. "Carli kind of modeled it for them, and together they made a to-do list on the students' desks before she sent them off to do independent work," Kristin described. To keep students moving closer to the goal, Carli kept checking with the kids, and "they would be accountable for answering to her." That effort moved time on task to 72%.

Carli then came up with the idea that every student should have a learning buddy they could go to if they had questions. "Carli," Kristin said, "strategically partnered students with someone who was mostly on task the whole time. Each student had a sort of expert they could go to in order to help each other get back on track." That moved time on task to 87%.

Carli and Kristin were both thrilled when they hit the goal (they actually exceeded it) because they "really could see a marked difference with behavior and learning." The students were producing more "quality work." Even though these were just "small tweaks," they made a big difference. "The growth revealed in the data affirmed who Carli was as a teacher. You could see her confidence grow. She felt like she was doing it right," Kristin noted.

Engagement data, like those Kristin gathered for Carli, make up an essential part of improvement. Data are used to set goals, to see how well strategies are working, to monitor progress, and to celebrate success. We believe engagement data, the type Kristin gathered in Carli's class, are particularly important because engagement stands at the very heart of a meaningful life.

There is ample evidence to show that engagement is important for many aspects of a well-lived life. When Mihaly Csikszentmihalyi (1990) did an exhaustive study of optimal living, for example, he concluded that engagement was central to happiness. A happy person is an engaged person. Similarly, John Gottman (2001) found that engagement, which he referred to as emotional connection, was essential for healthy relationships. People in healthy relationships engage with their partners by noticing and responding to their partner's bids for connection. And when Jim Loehr and Tony Schwartz wrote about the high-performing individuals they studied at LGE Performance Systems, they called their book *The Power of Full Engagement* (2003). Engagement, they concluded, is the defining characteristic of highly successful people.

In any life, then, engagement is important for happiness, relationships, and productivity, and, not surprisingly, engagement is critically important for students to succeed in school. Readers can't know what is in a book unless they open it up and read the words on the pages. In the same way, students who aren't paying attention won't learn from their teacher or classmates. Engagement is unquestionably an *a priori* condition for learning.

Student engagement is also the critical factor for keeping students in educational organizations. Students who don't feel like they belong in school or don't feel connected to school are students who are at risk for dropping out (e.g., Dary et al., 2016; Rumberger et al., 2017). If we want equitable schools, where all students have an equal chance to succeed, we need to create schools where students are engaged.

Engagement is much more than students sitting up straight and keeping quiet in class. In fact, if students focus too much on looking like they are learning, they may be distracted from actually learning. To define engagement, we distinguish between three categories: behavioral, cognitive, and emotional. Behavioral engagement refers to how students act during a class—do they look like they are learning? Cognitive engagement refers to how students process learning experiences—is their learning experience producing what their teacher had in mind for them? Finally, emotional engagement refers to how students feel about their experiences in school—do they feel positive, hopeful, and connected; do they feel like they belong? Each of these categories of engagement, including several kinds of engagement within each category, and ways of gathering the different kinds of engagement data are described below.

Behavioral Engagement

When students are behaviorally engaged, they look engaged. If the teacher is talking, students are looking at the teacher. Behaviorally engaged students ask and answer questions and appear to be completing assignments and doing what their teacher asks them to do. When students aren't behaviorally engaged, on the other hand, they don't fully participate in classroom activities. They do other things, such as play with their phone, have side conversations, disrupt other students, disrupt the teacher, and so forth.

Uses

Behavioral engagement data are a helpful kind of data to gather when behavior is a major issue in a class. A second advantage of behavioral engagement is that they can be gathered easily and reliably. For this reason, researchers often choose to measure behavioral engagement data for research studies.

Limitations

Behavioral engagement data shine a light on how students are acting, but they don't tell us a lot about what is happening in students' minds and hearts. As any teacher can tell you, just because a student looks like she is learning doesn't mean she is learning. Behavioral data, then, are very helpful when behavior is a major issue in a classroom, but they don't give us a complete picture of student learning and well-being without connection to engagement.

Ways to Determine Behavioral Engagement

Time on Task

What is time on task? Time on task measures whether students look like they are doing what they are supposed to be doing during a lesson. Gathering data on time on task involves assessing whether students appear to be doing the task their teacher has asked them to do.

TIME ON TASK T-CHART

On Task	Not on Task
Appears to be doing the assigned activity	Appears to not be doing the assigned activity
Maintains eye contact with the teacher or learning partners	Does not maintain eye contact with the teacher or learning partners
Responds to the teacher's questions	Doesn't respond to the teacher's questions or response is off task
Is in their seat	Is out of their seat
Produces appropriate work for the assignment	Doesn't produce appropriate (or any) work for the assignment

Source: From *The Definitive Guide to Instructional Coaching* by Jim Knight, 2021.

HOW TO GATHER TIME-ON-TASK DATA

When observers gather time-on-task data, they are taking a sample of classroom behavior based on their objective observations—what school psychologists call "direct observable behavior." That is, they look at each student in a class, determine whether the student appears to be on task, note down their observation, and quickly move to the next student, repeating the process until they have observed all students in the class. Often observers gather time-on-task data every 5 or 10 minutes during a lesson to get a sample.

TIME ON TASK RESOURCES

Scan here for more information and research related to time on task.

The easiest way to record time-on-task data is to use a teacher's seating chart for her class. If the collaborating teacher has a seating chart available to share, you can use that, or you can quickly draw a chart if one isn't available. To code time on task, put plusses for "engaged" and minuses for "not engaged" for each student on the seating chart, as shown below. You should be able to code time on task for an entire class in a minute or two. We also suggest you note the time for each observation and what students were doing when you observed them.

If students are moving around a lot during a lesson and using a seating chart isn't feasible, you can draw a three-column table and then (a) write down the time of each observation, (b) note what students were doing, and (c) record plusses or minuses on the same line of the table as depicted on the second chart below.

When you gather time-on-task data, keep in mind that you are taking a sample of student behavior. If a student is almost always on task but happens to appear to be off task when you look at them, record what you see. Collecting this kind of data is like taking a picture—it's a snapshot of time—rather than recording a video, which produces more context and lengthier interactions. Only report what you see students doing at the moment you look at them. What you see, as they say, is what you get.

TIME ON TASK (USING A SEATING CHART)

Time on Task			

+ + + – Chelsea	+ + + – Moriah	+ + + + Maya	+ + + + Idris
+ + + + Jacobe	+ + – – Rylee	+ – – – Kai	

+ – + + Aya	+ + + + Dylan	+ + + – Ko	+ + + + Dara
+ – + + Jayden	+ + + + Annalise	+ + + + Preston	

+ – + – Isabel	+ + – + Luca	+ – – – Nora	+ + + + Gabriel
– – – – Malik	– + – + Raleigh		+ – + + + Eunice

TIME	INSTRUCTIONAL PRACTICE	STUDENTS IN CLASS	STUDENTS ON TASK	PERCENTAGE
8:15	Review	21	20	95%
8:25	Describe	21	14	67%
8:35	Model	21	16	76%
8:45	Practice	21	13	61%
			Total Average	75%

TIME ON TASK (NO SEATING CHART)

8:15 Review
20/21 = 95%

```
+ + + - + + + + + + + + + + + +
+ + +
```

8:25 Describe
14/21 = 67%

```
+ + + - + + - + + - + - - + + +
- + - +
```

8:35 Model
16/21 = 76%

```
+ + + - + + + + + - + + - + + + -
+ - +
```

8:45 Practice
13/21 = 61%

```
+ - - + - + + - + + - + + + - + + +
- + -
```

Total Average: 75%

PRO TIP

Partner with your collaborating teacher to create a decision rule you can apply whenever you're not sure whether a student is on or off task. You might ask the teacher, "If I'm not sure if a student is on task, what do you think is most likely?" Then each time you're uncertain whether a student is or isn't on task, you can apply the decision rule based on what your teacher said is most likely. What matters here is that you are always consistent with your observations so that the teacher can compare data recorded the same way at different points over time.

Productive Time

What is productive time? During any lesson, time either will or will not be used productively. We've yet to see a lesson where every second was focused on student growth in some way. Students need to pull out their textbooks or pencils, move from one activity to the next, or settle in to learn after the bell has sounded. In some situations, there is so much unproductive time that it ends up decreasing learning. For example, we have observed lessons where 20%, 30%, or more of the lesson is unproductive time. Functionally, that totals to more than seven weeks of lost learning time during one school year!

During unproductive time, students transition between activities, pack up to leave before the end of class, get assignments from their lockers, talk after the bell, and so forth. Having said that, all instructional time doesn't have to be focused on learning outcomes to be considered productive. As the T-chart below explains, productive time may be time spent connecting current events to learning in class or talking about how prepared students are for learning, community-building activities, or many other activities that contribute to creating a learning community even though they are not directly related to the learning goals in the class.

PRODUCTIVE TIME T-CHART

Nonexamples	Examples
Settling in before the bell	Students are discussing how prepared they are to learn
Transitioning between activities	Teacher offering instructions on effective learning behavior
Pulling out materials such as a textbook	Negative nonverbal communication
Discussing current events that are unrelated to learning in class	Discussing how learning applies to real life
Packing up before the bell at the end of class	Discussing current events that are related to learning in class

Source: From *The Definitive Guide to Instructional Coaching* by Jim Knight, 2021.

PRODUCTIVE TIME

See QR code for more information research related to productive time.

HOW TO GATHER DATA ON PRODUCTIVE (AND UNPRODUCTIVE) TIME

Data on productive and unproductive time are easy to gather. You might want to use a form such as the one included below, but all you really need is a pen, some paper, and a smartphone (or stopwatch). Start by noting the time when you started observing how time is used in the classroom. Then, each time the class is unproductive, use your timer to apply the definition of productive time developed by you and the cooperating teacher to keep track of the total unproductive time. Then, when learning is productive, write down the amount of total productive time on your notepad or in the productive column on the form. For example, if the bell to start class rings at 10:00 and it takes 4 minutes and 23 seconds for the lesson to start, you would note 4:23 on your notepad.

Keep recording and noting unproductive time whenever the class is unproductive. Note when you stop observing the class. Then to calculate productive and unproductive time, record the total amount of time of the observation and subtract total unproductive time. The leftover time is the amount of productive time. For example, if the observation is 40 minutes long, and unproductive (noninstructional) time is 15 minutes, then total productive time is 25 minutes (40 − 15 = 25). We have found that teachers are frequently surprised at how much unproductive time occurs when they reflect on their data. Sometimes unproductive time ranges between 20–30% of class time.

PRODUCTIVE TIME

Productive	Unproductive
Total Time:	Total Time:

Other Aspects of Instructional Time

Educators can also learn a lot by taking a more precise look at other aspects of instructional time. For example, an observer could use a table similar to the one below to note the time dedicated to the different ways students were engaged during a lesson. Since the learning activities during any lesson will vary, observers shouldn't limit their observations to the variables included below and should talk with the collaborating teacher about what variables the teacher would like to have recorded.

ASSESSING INSTRUCTIONAL TIME Date:

Observation Begins:

Observation Ends:

Learning Activity	Time
Unproductive Time	
Direct Instruction	
Small Group	
Discussion	
Teacher Modeling	
Independent Practice	
Warm-Up	
Tests/Quizzes	
Silent Reading	
Review	

Depicting Instructional Time Data

Instructional time data can be depicted through a spreadsheet, a bar graph for each variable, a pie chart, and no doubt other ways. We have found that pie charts, such as the one shown below, are especially helpful because they depict the entire class and each of the learning experiences in one easy-to-grasp chart.

INSTRUCTIONAL TIME

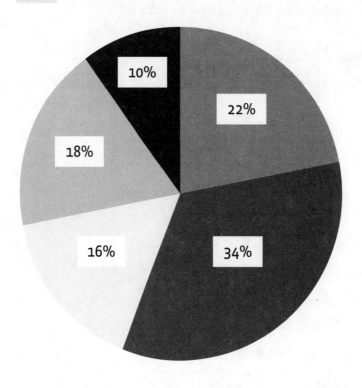

Learning Variable	Time	%	Key
Unproductive Time	11	22	
Direct Instruction	17	34	
Teacher Modeling	8	16	
Independent Practice	9	18	
Review	5	10	
Total	50	100	

Engagement-Time Index (the ETI)

The Engagement-Time Index (ETI) combines two forms of data—time on task and productive time—to produce one number that provides quick, big-picture insight into what is happening in a classroom.

LIMITATIONS

The ETI shines a light on simple ways to increase student learning, but it is only one tool, and it does not measure the relevance, quality, depth, or impact of the learning occurring. As a result, it is important to use it along with other ways of reviewing what is happening in the classroom.

HOW TO CALCULATE THE ETI

To calculate the ETI, write the percentages for time on task and productive time as decimals (e.g., 70% learning time becomes .70 and 70% time on task becomes .70). Then multiply the two numbers, .70 × .70 = .49, showing that slightly less than half was engaged, productive time. The ETI's simplicity helps teachers see patterns that otherwise might remain invisible.

PRO TIP

Observers should practice gathering data on productive and unproductive time separately, perhaps by conducting observations with a colleague and comparing notes, before calculating the ETI.

Disruptions

Disruptions are student actions that interrupt a teacher's instruction or students' learning. Disruptions here do not include disruptive announcements that come over the school's PA system (although gathering those data could be informative). As the T-chart below suggests, disruptions include such actions as students blurting out answers, having side conversations, getting out of their seat, bothering other students, and so forth.

LIMITATIONS

When observers gather disruption data as we describe them, they do not assess the seriousness of the disruption. Obviously, when a student makes a disruptive joke about content being discussed in class, it's not as serious as a student throwing their desk across the classroom. For this reason, observers may want to enhance their data gathering by taking notes about significant disruptions students make during a lesson.

DISRUPTIONS T-CHART

Examples	Nonexamples
Blurting out answers to questions	Disruptions over the PA
Having side conversations	Asking for help
Bothering other students	Engaging in negative nonverbal communication
Out of their seat	Sleeping in class
Arguing with the teacher	Looking out the window

HOW TO GATHER DISRUPTIONS DATA

Observers can gather disruption data in much the same way as time on task, as illustrated in the chart below. Using a teacher's seating chart, or one you have created yourself for the observation, each time a student disrupts the class, put tally marks on the box representing that student. Note the time when the observation began and ended so that you can calculate a "number of disruptions per 10 minutes" score. For example, if the observation is 20 minutes long, and if there are 16 disruptions during those 20 minutes, the number of disruptions per 10 minutes would be 8. Calculating the number of disruptions per 10 minutes is useful since teachers may want to set a goal of no more than, say, 2 or 3 disruptions per 10 minutes, and the observational data will help the teacher assess whether or not their strategy is actually decreasing the number of disruptions.

Decreasing disruptions is a popular goal when teachers want to increase behavioral engagement. When students are disruptive, they interrupt other students who are trying to learn, and they add to teachers' stress. Most teachers find it difficult to be clear, supportive, and inspirational when students are constantly disrupting their teaching.

MEASURING DISRUPTIONS

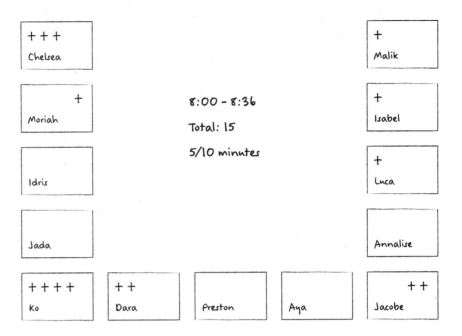

Responses

A final kind of behavioral engagement data to measure is how students respond to questions. In particular, for behavioral engagement, observers can note how often students respond, how many different students respond, or both. Observers can also gather data on how frequently students give correct responses and the level of student responses, but since these two types of data are more related to cognitive engagement, we will talk about them in the cognitive engagement section later in this chapter.

When students are engaged, they usually answer questions asked by the teacher. Indeed, during direct instruction, one way to increase engagement is to increase the number of opportunities to respond—more on this in Chapter 7. Data on responses can also reveal information about which students are or are not answering questions. For example, an observer might keep track of the number of boys and girls answering questions or the number of first-language English speakers answering questions compared with multilinguistic students and so forth. When educators look at response data, they gain insight into how and who their lessons are engaging or not engaging.

LIMITATIONS

We would be incorrect to assume that students aren't engaged if they aren't answering questions. Students process information in their own way, and for some students, responding in class may not help them learn content. A student could be learning and applying all the knowledge, skills, and concepts offered in a class even though they do not want to answer questions in class.

HOW TO GATHER RESPONSE DATA

Observers can gather data on student responses in the same way they gather time-on-task or disruption data, by using the seating chart and putting a mark on the page in the space designated for each student. The seating chart below is an example of how the form might be used.

MEASURING RESPONSES

+ + + + Chelsea	+ + + Idris
+ + Moriah	+ + Jada

8:06 – 8:36

Total responses: 26

OTR > 1/min

9/20

+ + Malik	+ + + Eunice
 Raleigh	

 Annalise	+ + + + + Luca
 Jacobe	 Isabel

+ + + Ko	 Dara
 Preston	 Aya

 Gabriel	+ + Porter
 Tyler	

Teachers can learn about how their questions affect students' responses by video recording lessons with the camera pointed away from the teacher and toward students. Even though they are not in the video, teachers can hear their questions and see immediately what impact they had on different students.

Cognitive Engagement

As we have seen, the data gathered for behavioral engagement focus on whether students look like they are learning—essentially, what observers see students doing. In contrast, cognitive engagement focuses on what happens inside students—essentially, whether students really are experiencing a learning activity the way their teachers hope they'll experience it. When we measure cognitive engagement, therefore, we are really assessing the impact learning activities have on students.

Phil Schlechty's (2011) pioneering work describing types of engagement is helpful here. Schlechty explained that students can be *authentically engaged, strategically compliant,* or *not engaged.* Not engaged is easy to understand. Students are not doing what their teacher wants them to be doing. Strategically compliant students, in turn, are doing what they are supposed to be doing, not because the activity is important to them, but for a strategic reason. For example, they may be compliant because they want to get a good grade, they don't want to disappoint the teacher, or they don't want the teacher to call their parents about their behavior.

We see Schlechty's authentic engagement as quite similar to our view of cognitive engagement, so we chose to use the more common term *cognitive engagement.* When students are cognitively engaged, they are getting out of the activity what their teacher wants them to get out of it (and perhaps even more than the teacher intended).

Limitations

Cognitive engagement sounds like the kind of engagement we want for our students, so why wouldn't we focus on gathering this kind of data? The problem is that in order to understand what is happening inside students, you need to ask them to tell you, and students, like all people, do not always give reliable reports of their behavior.

How to Gather Cognitive Engagement Data

One way to gather cognitive engagement data is by using an experience sampling form like the one included below (for more information on experience sampling, see Hektner et al., 2006). When you use experience sampling forms, give a form to each student. Then set a timer (such as a digital kitchen timer or one that will silently vibrate) to go off every 10 minutes. Tell students to circle their level of engagement from 1 to 6 (with 1 representing not engaged and 6 representing fully engaged) when the timer goes off. At the end of class, ask students to write down any comments they have about how the class could be made more engaging for them and collect their forms.

We have found that the form works well when students are behaviorally engaged, but we don't suggest using the form with students who are off task or disruptive. Even if students are merely strategically compliant, they will complete the form without it interrupting their learning. Students who are not behaviorally engaged, however, may use the form as another reason to be off task.

 PRO TIP

If you video or audio record a lesson, then review the forms with the video recording nearby. You can then slide the recording to the point when the timer goes off to see what students were doing right before they circled a number on the form. Reflect on the actual level of reported student engagement in comparison to your own perception of engagement at that point in the lesson.

Responses

Two other kinds of data that tell us about cognitive engagement are (a) correct academic responses and (b) level of responses.

ENGAGEMENT FORM

Date:

INSTRUCTIONS: Each time you hear the bell, please rate how engaging the learning activity is for you.

Bell	Non-engaged		Compliant			Engaged
1	1	2	3	4	5	6
2	1	2	3	4	5	6
3	1	2	3	4	5	6
4	1	2	3	4	5	6
5	1	2	3	4	5	6
6	1	2	3	4	5	6
7	1	2	3	4	5	6
8	1	2	3	4	5	6
9	1	2	3	4	5	6
10	1	2	3	4	5	6
11	1	2	3	4	5	6
12	1	2	3	4	5	6

Correct Academic Responses

As with many other forms of data gathering, you can gather data on correct academic responses (CARs) with quick marks on a form. Mark a plus for a correct response or a minus for an incorrect response.

Please note that an extremely high percentage of correct responses (say 98%) isn't always the best. When people are learning, they often need to make mistakes, so an incorrect response may actually show us that students are taking risks and learning. Research supports keeping the rate of correct responses around 80% during guided practice and above 90% when students engage in independent practice (Reinke, 2011).

STUDENT ENGAGEMENT AND SELF-REPORTING

See QR code for more information on student engagement and self-reporting.

LEVEL OF RESPONSE

One way to assess the quality of student responses is to look at the learning level. There are many ways to do this. The most popular way to assess the level of students' responses is likely Benjamin Bloom's seminal taxonomy of academic outcomes, first developed in the 1950s. When you apply Bloom's taxonomy, you note whether a student's response is at the knowledge, comprehension, application, analysis, synthesis, or evaluation level. In 2001, Lorin Anderson, David Krathwohl and their colleagues published a revised version of Bloom's taxonomy that identifies remembering, understanding, applying, analyzing, evaluating, and creating as their learning levels. Other ways to look at students' responses include John Biggs's and Kevin Collis's SOLO Taxonomy (1982) and Norman Webb's Depth of Knowledge (DOK) framework (see Francis, 2021).

When instructional coaches who partnered with Jim tried to use Bloom's taxonomy (Bloom, 1956) to gather data on questions, they found it challenging to describe and apply fluently. Eventually, Jim's team landed on three levels, which are described in Chapter 7—content knowledge (simply described as knowledge), procedural knowledge (skills), and conceptual knowledge (big ideas).

PRO TIP

Whatever framework an observer adopts, we have two suggestions. First, we highly recommend that the observer and teacher spend some time ensuring that they have a shared understanding of the levels within the framework, regardless of whether it is old Bloom, new Bloom, SOLO, DOK, or knowledge, skills, and big ideas. A shared understanding of what data are being gathered is important for any observation, but given the complexity of the various levels within the above frameworks, it is especially important when gathering data on the level of student responses.

Second, we recommend that the observer write down all individual student responses during a lesson. Then the observer and teacher can go through the list and code the level of each response together later.

Emotional Engagement

What is emotional engagement? When students are emotionally engaged, they feel safe, positive, that they have hope about their academic futures and that they belong in school. When we discuss emotional engagement in our workshops, educators often tell us they think emotional engagement is a necessary prerequisite for any kind of learning to take place.

Ways to Measure Emotional Engagement

The concept of emotional engagement is one people grasp quickly, but the specific, measurable components making up emotional engagement are more difficult to define. Martin Seligman's list of the elements of well-being, which he describes in *Flourish* (2011), provides one way of thinking about emotional engagement. If we live a "flourishing" life, Seligman writes, we have positive experiences, we are engaged, our experiences are meaningful, and we feel a sense of accomplishment. He organizes these variables using the acronym PERMA. Other psychologists have added health to the acronym to denote whether or not we are living in healthy ways (Kern, 2022).

SELIGMAN'S ELEMENTS OF WELL-BEING

Positive Emotion

Engagement

Relationships

Meaning

Accomplishment

Source: Adapted from *Flourish* by Martin Seligman, 2011.

Limitations

As is the case with cognitive engagement, educators must rely on self-report to gather emotional engagement data. Certainly, what students say and do in class can shed some light on student engagement, but if we really want to understand how students are feeling, we need to ask them, and that means that any data we gather will be unreliable. First, students may not have a clear understanding of their emotional state. Most people struggle at times to describe how they're feeling (Brackett, 2019). Second, students may not be comfortable telling others about their emotional state. Even when comments are confidential, students need to trust the data gatherer before they will share exactly how they're feeling. Finally, since data are gathered in an educational context where students are graded, students may be less forthright about their emotional state if they feel it will make them look like they are not good students.

How to Gather Data on Emotional Engagement

Despite the limitations of self-report data, we believe that imperfect data are better than no data. That said, the data must be valid and helpful, of course. Therefore, we offer several suggestions for how to measure emotional engagement.

INTERVIEWS

It is difficult to interview students frequently enough to see change, so interview data by themselves likely won't be an effective way of measuring progress toward a goal. However, if time permits, interviewing a sample of students about their emotional engagement can help educators better understand their students' emotional state. Interviews can be conducted by teachers, if students have learning activities that the teacher doesn't have to directly supervise; otherwise, it can be done by coaches, administrators (if a teacher wishes), or even by colleagues. Teachers can take turns interviewing students in each other's classes and then discuss what they heard in the interviews. Although the questions should be tailored to the unique students in a given teacher's classroom, Gallup's Student Success Survey (2020), for example, includes nine statements that may be adapted and used as questions for interviews related to emotional engagement.

SAMPLE ENGAGEMENT POLL

I have close friends at school.

This school makes me feel secure.

My schoolwork is important.

I get to use my strengths daily.

Teachers frequently praise my good effort.

I feel like my opinion matters in this school.

Source: Adapted from GallupStudentPoll.com.

Another option is to use questions stemming from Martin Seligman's acronym PERMA (2011), listed below.

PERMA QUESTIONS

Positive Emotion. How happy and satisfied were you last week?

Engagement. How often were you completely engaged in learning activities in this class last week?

Relationships. How positive were your interactions with other people last week?

Meaning. How meaningful were your experiences last week?

Accomplishment. How proud are you of what you accomplished last week?

Finally, research on hope (Lopez & Sidhu, 2013) provides another way to ask students about their engagement.

HOPE QUESTIONS

Goal: What is your goal for next week in this class?

Pathways: What are you going to do to hit your goal?

Agency: How confident are you that you will hit your goal?

RESEARCH ON HOPE

See QR code for more information related to research on hope.

EXIT TICKETS

Another simple and powerful way to gather data on emotional engagement is through the use of exit tickets that students complete during class. Often exit tickets are handed out just before the end of class, but given the reflective nature of commenting on emotions, you may want to give these tickets at the start of class. Teachers who want to gauge how students' emotional engagement evolves during a semester can give the same exit ticket once a week. Secondary-level students can complete exit tickets with a Likert scale, and students in elementary grades can complete an exit ticket with emoticons. Teachers can also prompt students to include information about (a) how they are feeling, (b) what they want the teacher to know about them, or (c) how the class can be improved. Teachers who are engaged in impact cycles (see Chapter 4) can set goals for improvement based on students' responses on exit tickets. Several example exit tickets are included at the end of this chapter.

INTERACTIVE JOURNALS

You can also gather data on students' emotional engagement using digital or paper journals. Students can be given time once or twice a week to journal about their emotional state, and then teachers can respond in the journals with words of support, encouragement, or praise. By writing back and forth to each other in a journal, students and teachers can build a one-to-one connection that might not otherwise be possible in a class with many students. One disadvantage of such journaling is that reading and responding to 150 journals each week (as might be the case in some middle schools) would take more time than most teachers have available. Also, journaling isn't anonymous, and not all students will be forthcoming with thoughts about their emotional state if they know that their teachers will read the words knowing who wrote them.

Although some students may not be completely open about their emotional state, one thing we have found is that when you ask students how they feel, more often than not they will tell you, and educators should be prepared to hear some hard things about students' experiences. Not knowing how students feel may make it easier to stay on track with a pacing guide, but avoiding that reality doesn't help us reach students. When teachers gather data on emotional engagement, they are presented with an opportunity to have a profoundly positive impact—in some cases, they may even save a student's life.

PRO TIP

Some schools assess emotional engagement schoolwide, and we suggest schools consider doing this as a point of departure for conversations about meeting students' needs. When everyone in the school has a deeper understanding of students' perceptions of their emotional needs, that knowledge can lead to changes that help create schools where students really feel like they belong.

To Sum Up

———

Engagement is an important outcome in schools because engagement is a central part of happiness, healthy relationships, and productivity. Additionally, students can't learn, and often drop out of school, when they aren't engaged. In this chapter we discussed three categories of engagement data: behavioral, cognitive, and emotional engagement.

Making It Real

———

Students

Students can provide a lot of important data that can be a part of an Impact Cycle. For example, exit tickets can provide insight into students' emotional states and provide an opportunity for students to share suggestions on what would help them learn. Teachers need to ensure that students have an accurate understanding of the purpose and use of the data they are sharing before students complete experience sampling, exit tickets, or other ways of sharing their level of engagement. Otherwise, we risk students trivializing the opportunity to have a voice in the process—something they are far too likely to have experienced in the past.

Teachers

Teachers can gather a lot of important data directly from students, as mentioned above. Also, they can gather a lot of data by reviewing video of their lessons to see which students are responding to questions or are disruptive, or to notice the amount of productive time or other instructional time variables related to the classroom.

Coaches

Some forms of data are difficult for teachers to see on video or during teaching. For example, we have found that time-on-task data are difficult to score on video. In many cases, teachers prefer to focus on teaching and learning, letting coaches gather data on such things as disruptions or responses. Whatever kind of data is gathered, coaches will have an invaluable role partnering with teachers to review data, set goals, determine progress, and identify next steps during an Impact Cycle.

Administrators

Conversations about data between administrators and teachers will be much more successful when teachers determine what data will be gathered. If this isn't possible, then it is crucial that administrators and teachers have a shared understanding of the kind(s) of data that are going to be gathered and why. We suggest administrators meet with teachers to confirm a mutual understanding of the kind(s) of data to be gathered and why those data are important.

 ## Going Deeper

Jim learned about the power of engagement data after partnering with Randy Sprick and Wendy Reinke in 2005 to explore coaching and classroom management. Randy's *CHAMPS* (1998) is an excellent book about how to measure and increase behavioral engagement in schools. Tricia Skyles's book *Coaching CHAMPS* (2022), which she wrote with Randy and Jim, takes Randy's ideas about engagement data and strategies and integrates them with instructional coaching. Any coach who is interested in increasing engagement will benefit greatly from Tricia's book.

Further, Phil Schlechty's *Engaging Students* (2011) helped us understand many of the nuances of student engagement in schools. We also highly recommend *Engagement by Design* (2017) by Doug Fisher, Nancy Frey, Russ Quaglia, Dominique Smith, and Lisa Lande, which is packed with useful information about how to increase student engagement.

Additional Forms for Gathering Data

On the following pages we have included additional forms to aid you in gathering data in the classroom.

Source: High-Impact Instruction: A Framework for Great Teaching, by Jim Knight. Thousand Oaks, CA: Corwin, www.corwin.com. Copyright © 2013 Corwin Press.

I feel happy today.

I'd feel happier if:

_____

_____

_____

_____

_____

_____

_____

_____

_____

_____

_____

_____

_____

_____

_____

_____

_____

happiness

I was happy today.

1	2	3	4	5	6
Not at all					Totally

What would have to change to make you happier?

_____

_____

_____

_____

_____

_____

_____

_____

_____

_____

_____

_____

_____

_____

_____

_____

_____

_____

happiness

I feel comfortable speaking in class.

1	2	3	4	5	6
Never					Always

What could be changed to make it easier for you to speak in class?

_____

_____

_____

_____

_____

_____

_____

_____

_____

_____

_____

_____

_____

_____

_____

_____

_____

openness

What are your goals for the week?

_____

_____

_____

_____

_____

What strategies will you use to meet your goals?

_____

_____

_____

_____

_____

How confident are you that you will meet your goal?

| 1 | 2 | 3 | 4 | 5 | 6 |
| Not confident | | | | | Very confident |

How can I help you hit your goals?

_____

_____

_____

_____

_____

hope

Today's lesson was meaningful.

1	2	3	4	5	6
Not at all					Totally

What could I change to make it more meaningful?

_____

_____

_____

_____

_____

_____

_____

_____

_____

_____

_____

_____

_____

_____

_____

_____

_____

_____

meaning

ACHIEVEMENT

|

is about

↓

gathering data that show
teachers and students how well
they are learning

*by
defining*

*by
clarifying*

*by
unpacking*

*by
assessing
with*

Knowledge

Learning

What
Students
Need
to Learn

Data Tools

- Selected response
- Brief constructed responses
- Checks for understanding
- Correct academic responses
- Single-point rubrics
- Analytic rubrics
- Interviews

CHAPTER 6

ACHIEVEMENT

Learning is, of course, the point of it all. In this chapter we describe how to gather data on whether or not students are learning. To do that, we describe how to become clear on what students are going to learn, define levels and kinds of learning, and present a variety of tools you can use to assess the different kinds and levels of learning. You can skip the first part of this chapter if you're an expert on curriculum development, but even so, you'll likely need to review the sections on how to assess the levels and kinds of learning.

CHAPTER RESOURCES

Access charts, diagrams, research, and resources from this chapter.

The beautiful thing about learning is that nobody can take it away from you.

B. B. KING

A few years ago, Jim visited Wendy Hopf, a highly accomplished 7th grade language arts teacher in a middle school in Philadelphia. Jim was there to record a course for the Teaching Channel, and after spending the day watching Wendy teach, he was curious to learn what Wendy would say had led to her teaching success. Jim asked her, "If a new teacher came into your classroom and asked you for advice, what would you tell her?"

After thinking for a few seconds, Wendy answered that she thought it was important that she had planned out "every single aspect of her curriculum" before the start of the year. Also, she said, it was important that she shared the curriculum with her students "all the time … [so] they get the idea of where this is going [and] what they're going to be expected to do." Finally, after reflecting, Wendy added, "I think it's a big communication piece … this is where we're going. So, if you know your curriculum, that's really key."

Knowing your curriculum is "key," as Wendy said, not just for teaching effectively but for gathering achievement data. You have to know what your students are supposed to learn before you start assessing whether or not they've learned it. However, knowing your curriculum is not as easy as it sounds. To that end, there are several important questions educators should ask.

First off, how do we define knowledge? Second, what do students do when they are learning? Third, how can teachers unpack what it is students must learn during each unit? Fourth, once we're clear on what we mean by knowing and learning, and clear on what students need to learn in a unit, how do we measure that learning?

Finally, how do we ensure that the assessment we choose is appropriate for the level and kind of learning we're assessing? Our answers to each of these questions are presented in this chapter.

How Do We Define Knowledge?

This question is not easily answered. Philosophers in the field of epistemology like Thomas Aquinas, Francis Bacon, and Rene Descartes have talked and written about knowledge for centuries and that conversation does not seem likely to end soon. For our practical purposes, we offer a working definition, dividing knowledge into three levels: knowledge, skills, and big ideas.

Knowledge (aka Content Knowledge)

We refer to the factual knowledge that students need to know to succeed in a discipline as content knowledge or, more simply, knowledge. When students are learning math facts, parts of speech, or the seven steps of the scientific method, they are learning content knowledge.

Skills (aka Procedural Knowledge)

When students learn how to do something, they are acquiring procedural knowledge, which we simply refer to as skills. Skills involve actions such as identifying, summarizing, editing, remembering, and paraphrasing. When students learn how to draw a vanishing point in a drawing, edit a text, break down an assignment, or learn the steps to outlining an essay, they are learning skills.

Big Ideas (aka Conceptual Knowledge, Higher-Order Thinking, Problem Solving, Evaluating, Creating)

We use the term *big ideas* to refer to learning that involves understanding concepts, seeing connections between concepts, and using higher-order thinking. For example, when students are learning how to compare and contrast the characteristics of reptiles and mammals, problem solve, evaluate, or create, they are learning big ideas.

What Do Students Do When They Are Learning?

_____

This is another big question that educators have discussed for some time. As we mentioned in Chapter 5, helpful suggestions have been provided by several authors, including Bloom and colleagues (1956), who offered the famous taxonomy of learning objectives—knowledge, comprehension, application, analysis, synthesis, and evaluation—Anderson and colleagues (2001), who reworked Bloom—remember, understand, apply, analyze, evaluate, create—and Webb's Depth of Knowledge (DOK) levels—recall, application, strategic thinking, and critical thinking (see Francis, 2022).

These authors all provide helpful information, and educators who read their work will broaden and deepen their understanding of what students are doing when they are learning. In this chapter, we use the ACT model, developed by Julie Stern and colleagues (2021), to distinguish kinds of learning.

In the ACT model, _A_ stands for acquisition, which measures whether students can recall a concept or concepts. _C_ stands for connect, which assesses whether or not students can connect concepts. _T_ stands for transfer, which measures whether or not students can transfer information to new settings. The more we can coach students to ... [transfer knowledge]," Stern (2021) writes, "the more flexible and creative their problem-solving abilities will be, and the more primed they will be to innovate" (p. 18). This kind of learning is essential, Stern argues, because "students need to understand conceptual relationships within and across disciplines to tackle our world's most pressing problems" (p. 19).

How Can Teachers Unpack What It Is Students Must Learn During Each Unit?

_____

Educators create better questions when they clearly understand and communicate the level(s) of knowledge and the kind(s) of learning they want their students to achieve. That is why Wendy Hopf, mentioned earlier in the chapter, used guiding questions to plan out, as she said, "every detail" of her curriculum. We suggest educators unpack what and how their students need to learn by creating guiding questions and specific proficiencies, which are described below.

Step One: Guiding Questions

Educators who want to create guiding questions, as Wendy Hopf did, should write four to six guiding questions for each unit they plan to teach. Guiding questions guide teachers as they determine the knowledge, skills, and big ideas they want students to learn during a unit. After they've been shared with students, guiding questions also guide students as they encounter the learning opportunities in teachers' classrooms, experiencing alignment and consistency between learning objectives, activities, and assessments. In the end, students who can completely and correctly answer all the questions for a unit should receive a high grade on the unit assessment. To create effective guiding questions, educators should consider the following characteristics.

GUIDING QUESTIONS MUST …

ADDRESS THE STANDARDS. Most districts and other educational organizations have in place a process for unpacking the standards, so we won't spend much time discussing this aspect of creating guiding questions. If you want to develop a deeper understanding of how teachers can unpack standards, we suggest you review Larry Ainsworth and Kira Donovan's *Rigorous Curriculum Design* (2019).

Ainsworth has many suggestions for addressing standards, but we think three are especially important. First, educators should go through the standards that guide their teaching and identify the nouns and verbs. Nouns usually describe knowledge; verbs usually describe skills. This is an important distinction because knowledge and skills, as we shall see, are usually assessed differently. Effective guiding questions point students to the important knowledge, skills, and big ideas they need to learn.

Second, Ainsworth suggests educators identify priority standards, the standards that all students need to learn. Teachers simply do not have enough time in the school year to effectively address each standard laid out in the documents created for learning in most settings. Indeed, we've heard several teachers say, "If I try to teach everything, nothing gets learned." Even in the most efficient classroom, therefore, some standards will have to be skipped or skimmed. For this reason, it is important that the most important standards, the ones that all students must meet, be identified.

Third, when educators consider the standards to be covered, they should think about the order in which different knowledge, skills, and big ideas need to be learned. Ainsworth refers to this sequencing of learning outcomes as a learning progression. We've written more about learning progressions and why they're especially helpful when gathering data below in the section on specific proficiencies.

ADDRESS THE CORRECT LEVEL OF KNOWLEDGE AND KIND OF LEARNING. For our purposes, we suggest distinguishing between knowledge, skills, and big ideas, as described above. In addition, we also suggest distinguishing between acquisition, connection, and transfer. Clarifying what and how students will learn (the level and kind of learning) is especially important for determining how to gather student achievement data.

DESCRIBE MEANINGFUL TOPICS. Educators write better guiding questions when they write them with their students in mind, asking themselves whether their students would find the learning they're describing to be meaningful or interesting. When educators determine that certain questions are not meaningful or interesting, they should revise them, as best they can, to create questions that are more compelling or meaningful. We realize that not every topic students are to learn is particularly compelling, but pausing to ask whether the learning can be expressed in a more meaningful or interesting way may lead to better guiding questions and better student learning.

BE CAREFUL WITH LANGUAGE. Since guiding questions describe what students are going to learn, they need to be written with care. This involves two factors. First, effective guiding questions must correctly describe the knowledge, skills, and big ideas students are to learn. Incorrect, vague, or imprecise questions may lead to incorrect, vague, or imprecise learning. At the same time, the primary audience for guiding questions is students, so questions must be written using vocabulary and sentence structure that is easy for students to understand. We suggest that questions be "non-translatable," which is to say, written in language that students understand immediately without any need for paraphrasing. Questions that are clear, correct, precise, and easy to understand are questions that help students learn.

PROMPT STUDENTS TO USE STRATEGIES, TECHNOLOGY, OR OTHER TOOLS AND SKILLS.
In any class, students will be expected to learn and apply learning strategies, technology, communication skills, or other kinds of learning. Students might, for example, be prompted to use an online service like Storybird to create and illustrate their writing, self-questioning reading strategies to enhance how well they understand what they read, or looping to improve how they listen to each other. If these practices are an important part of student learning, they should be included in the guiding questions.

What's most important about guiding questions is that they allude to all of the most important learning that will occur in a unit. We like to say that a good guiding question is like the tip of an iceberg, and just as the visible part of an iceberg is connected to something much larger, so too do guiding questions point toward all the knowledge, skills, and big ideas to be learned in a unit.

Step Two: Specific Proficiencies

Once guiding questions have been created, the important and challenging work of creating specific proficiencies begins. Specific proficiencies break down answers to the guiding questions into sentences that precisely state the knowledge, skills, and big ideas students need to learn. In most cases, a specific proficiency describes a distinct component of student learning (such as a fact, skill, or concept) that can and likely should be assessed individually. Each specific proficiency is a partial answer to a guiding question, and teachers should keep writing proficiencies for each guiding question until the question is completely answered (Knight, 2013).

GUIDING QUESTION:

Which strategies can writers use to plan effectively?

SPECIFIC PROFICIENCIES:

Planning involves getting ideas out of your head.

Planning involves organizing ideas.

Brainstorming is writing down all the ideas you can think of about a topic.

Clustering is doodling with bubbles to get ideas out of your head about a topic.

Free writing is writing non-stop for five minutes or more.

Ideas can be organized by using a planning map, frame, or other tool.

Planning and organizing make writing more coherent.

Source: From *The Definitive Guide to Instructional Coaching* by Jim Knight, 2021.

Frequently, specific proficiencies serve as learning targets for lessons. Connie Moss and Susan Brookhart (2012) define learning targets as written statements that "guide learning. They describe, in language students understand, the lesson-sized chunk of information, skills, and reasoning processes that students will come to know deeply" (p. 3). They "are written from the students' point of view, [and are shared throughout lessons] so that students can use them to guide their own learning" (p. 3). Those who are creating learning targets, however, shouldn't feel that each proficiency must be a learning target. What matters is that the specific proficiencies precisely break down the knowledge, skills, or big ideas students need to understand.

Over the years, as we've worked with teachers, coaches, and administrators, we have found that the most effective specific proficiencies are (a) targeted, which is to say they provide a partial answer to a guiding question; (b) focused, containing one idea; (c) complete, written as a complete sentence; (d) short, as concise as possible; (e) accessible, easily understood by students; and (f) comprehensive, they represent a complete answer to a guiding question when combined with other specific proficiencies.

Effective Specific Proficiencies Are	✓
Targeted: a partial answer to a guiding question	
Focused: contain one idea	
Complete: written as a complete sentence	
Short: as concise as possible	
Accessible: easily understood by students	
Comprehensive: provide a complete answer to a guiding question when combined with other specific proficiencies	
Address categories of error that arose in the previous day's work	

Many educators have found it useful to list the specific proficiencies in the order in which students will be learning them, which Larry Ainsworth (2019) refers to as learning progressions. Identifying the order in which proficiencies will be learned is important, especially when combined with data gathering, because it helps teachers pinpoint exactly where students need help with their learning.

Discussing learning progressions with colleagues can help teachers deepen their understanding of the content, but creating learning progressions is, at best, an imperfect art. Educators need to think carefully about how their students learn; indeed, educators need to consider what it is they mean by "learning." Does a specific proficiency describe something students need to merely be aware of, or does it describe something students should never forget? Grant Wiggins and Jay McTighe (1998) refer to this kind of learning that students remember long after a lesson as enduring understandings:

> Enduring refers to the big ideas, the important understandings, that we
> want students to "get inside of" and retain after they've forgotten many

of the details ... Enduring understandings go beyond discrete facts or skills to focus on larger concepts, principles, or processes. (p. 10)

We have not found one right way to create specific proficiencies and guiding questions. Some educators like to fill stickies with their ideas about what students will learn in a unit and then organize the stickies into a group that they eventually synthesize into guiding questions and specific proficiencies. Others start by listing the sequence of their lessons, then listing the learning targets, and working their way back to the guiding questions. Yet other educators create learning maps for their units and then work backwards to create questions and proficiencies (for more information on learning maps, see Knight, 2013).

Over time, people will be able to decide what method works best for them. What seems to be universal, however, is that creating clear, effective guiding questions and then writing precise, easily understood specific proficiencies is challenging work. In a manner very similar to a poet trying to find the right words to point toward some ineffable part of life, educators sometimes struggle to find the right words for guiding questions and specific proficiencies. Like all creative acts, the struggle is real and the temptation is to give up. We hope you won't.

Steven Pressfield is a creativity expert whose ideas have been embraced by influential authors like Seth Godin and Ryan Holiday. In his and Shawn Coyne's book *War of Art* (2002), Pressfield describes creativity as an almost spiritual struggle between what we are trying to create, what we may even feel compelled to create, and what he labels as the resistance—all the various forces and reasons that keep us from doing our work. "Resistance," Pressfield writes, "cannot be seen, touched, heard, or smelled. But it can be felt. We experience it as an energy field radiating from a work-in-potential. It's a repelling force. It's negative. Its aim is to shove us away, distract us, prevent us from doing our work" (p. 7).

We're convinced that when teachers create guiding questions, specific proficiencies, or other curriculum documents or organizers, at times they experience resistance in exactly the same way. One way to move through this roadblock is to simply recognize the resistance and keep moving forward. A crappy first draft is better than no draft, and that less-than-perfect draft is a much more helpful starting place than nothing.

Like so much in life, the trick is to keep moving and improving until you're happy with what you've created. Your hard work will be rewarded by better learning experiences for your students.

How Do We Measure Student Learning?

Once educators are clear on what they want their students to learn, they need to determine how they will measure whether their students are learning. Student achievement data, when gathered effectively, are a powerful tool for increasing student learning and teacher efficacy. Also, achievement data are often used by educators to set goals and monitor progress. The Data Rules (see also Chapter 2) provide a lens for understanding what it means to gather achievement data effectively.

Rule #1: Foster Hope and Rule #2: Tied to Professional Learning

As we've mentioned throughout this book, data are most powerful when they foster hope, and as hope theorists Shane Lopez (2013) and Rick Snyder (2003) have written, hope involves three components: (a) something to hope for or a goal, (b) pathways to the goal, and (c) agency, belief that the pathway can take us to the goal.

When it comes to achievement data, then, educators will experience hope when data help them identify a clear goal, when that goal is tied to professional development that will help them see a pathway to the goal, and when frequently gathered data demonstrate that students are making progress toward the goal, thus building agency. The opposite is also true. When data are not tied to professional learning, and educators aren't able to see pathways to their goals, they can be left feeling helpless, frustrated, and defeated.

Rule #3: Chosen and Rule #8: Gathered by the Teacher

As we've mentioned earlier in this book, a common way for data to be gathered and shared is for an observer to visit a teacher's classroom and gather data on a form that the teacher did not choose and then share those data with the teacher. Such an approach to data gathering is likely necessary for teacher evaluation, but it is less effective when the data gathering is intended for professional learning (Buckingham & Goodall, 2019; Knight, 2023). We suggest, therefore, that the teacher, often in partnership with a coach or peer, identify the data to be gathered. We are more motivated to hit goals we set for ourselves (Heath & Heath, 2010) and more affected by data we gather and review ourselves.

Rule #4: Objective and Rule #5: Reliable and Mutually Understood

The best data accurately assess how well students acquire, connect, and transfer knowledge, skills, and big ideas. Good data are fair and free from bias. Therefore, directions and questions given to students on assessments should be clear and easy to understand. Educators can learn a lot by getting feedback from colleagues or friends on the clarity of questions and directions.

Rule #6: Valid

Data are only helpful if they assess what they are intended to assess. For example, a multiple-choice test on how to bake a souffle would not be as valid an assessment as actually watching someone bake a souffle. To ensure that their assessments are valid, educators need to think carefully about what they are assessing (is the knowledge being assessed content, procedural, or conceptual?) and what kind of assessment works best for the knowledge being assessed. In the case of the souffle, a rubric might be more valid than a selected-response test.

Rule #7: Frequently Gathered

When data are tied to professional learning, it helps educators see what is working and what isn't working. For this reason, data need to be gathered frequently. Often this means that students need to learn how to self-assess and share their progress so that they and their teacher know how well they are progressing. When students self-assess, they also learn an important part of learning how to learn.

Rule #9: Easy to Gather and Review

When it comes to anything we adopt or implement—an idea, a piece of technology, a kind of data—we are more likely to adopt it if it is valuable to us and easy to use (Csikszentmihalyi, 1994). The same applies to data. People are more likely to use data that are easy to gather and powerful, and when it comes to student achievement, powerful data tell us a lot about what students do and do not know.

Both of these variables—easy and powerful—are essential. A quick exit ticket about students' attitudes about writing might be easy to review, but if it doesn't reveal what students know and can do, then other assessments will be necessary. Also, a precise but complex rubric for writing might thrill a language arts teacher, like Jim or Mike, but it isn't much good if students find it so difficult to understand that they can't use it to improve their writing.

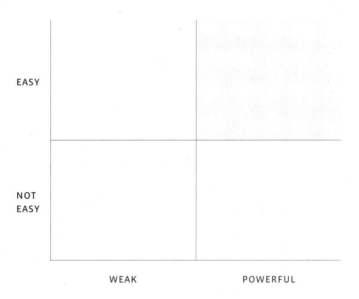

Rule #10: Validated by Research

As educators, we know that data can come from a variety of sources. In classrooms, teachers typically use formative and summative assessments to measure student progress and mastery of critical concepts. Additionally, diagnostic assessments that probe fundamental elements of skill development and screeners to indicate risk are valuable tools to further guide instructional decision making. Research consistently validates that a comprehensive model of schoolwide assessment planning that incorporates each of these elements is vital. However, of particular importance to improving student outcomes is careful educator analysis of student data at regular intervals, using visual representations (e.g., graphing), and timely feedback to ensure high rates of successful practice. Each of the achievement measures listed in this chapter provides a component of the schoolwide data necessary.

MORE ON VALIDATING WITH RESEARCH

Scan QR code for more information on research validating a variety of kinds of achievement measures.

Tools for Measuring Student Achievement

————

There are many tools educators can use to assess students' knowledge, skills, and big ideas. Several of the most popular tools are described below.

Selected Response

Selected-response tests, as the name suggests, are designed to assess what students know by giving them questions, a variety of possible answers for each question, and prompting them to choose the response they believe is correct. Selected-response assessments, such as multiple-choice or true/false tests, are likely the best-known method for gathering data on student achievement.

When writing selected-response questions, educators should try to use positive, clear language in the directions, questions, and possible answers. They should also be certain that there is only one correct answer for each question. Effective assessments are comprehensive but concise. Too long an assessment isn't helpful to the students taking the tests or the teacher grading them.

ADVANTAGES AND DISADVANTAGES

Selected-response tests provide a precise numerical score for each student. If the test is valid, this can be helpful for both students and teachers. These tests are also usually quite easy to grade, and engaging in discussions with students after the test is returned can be a rich opportunity for learning.

A major disadvantage of selected-response tests is that they reduce learning to a simple number and do not allow for assessing more complex learning. Many students feel like they want to talk back to a test when there is more than one answer that they see as arguably correct. Also, given their simplicity, selected-response tests are most effective for knowledge tests and less effective for skill and big idea assessments. Jay McTighe and Steve Ferrara (2021) write that critics of selected-response tests "express concerns that multiple-choice tests lead to 'multiple-choice' teaching, that is, a focus on acquisition of facts rather than an emphasis on understanding and the thoughtful application of knowledge (Darling-Hammond & Adamson, 2013; Wiggins, 1992)" (p. 22).

PRO TIP

Teachers need to ensure that their assessments are bias-free. They can do this by using simple, clear, and inclusive language, avoiding stereotypes, and perhaps most important, thinking about the cultures and contexts within which their students live. Teachers can also learn a lot from discussing with colleagues and professional developers how to avoid bias during test construction. One of the best ways to improve the fairness and validity of assessments is to share them with colleagues, friends, and family members to see if they can identify changes that can be made to make assessments fair and clear.

Brief Constructed Responses

Brief constructed responses (often known as BCRs), as the name suggests, are assessments that give students a prompt, such as a question, and then invite them to answer the prompt. Educators can ask students to respond by writing a paragraph, a few sentences, or a few bullet points; by drawing a picture; by labeling a diagram; and so on.

As with selected-response assessments, BCRs should be clearly written and bias-free. Before writing BCRs, educators should ask a few questions to clarify the level and kind of learning they are assessing. Is this assessment designed to measure knowledge, skills, or big ideas? Is the assessment measuring acquisition, connection, or transfer (or some combination)? Educators should also think carefully about their criteria for grading.

ADVANTAGES AND DISADVANTAGES

BCRs are easier to grade than most single-point and analytic rubrics, but they are often more difficult to grade than selected-response tests. They often yield more information than multiple-choice tests, but their brevity means that they only reveal a small sample of learning. When they are used effectively, BCRs can be very helpful, but they have to be the right kind of assessment for the right kind of learning.

 PRO TIP

It can be helpful to give students explicit instructions on how long their responses should be. Teachers might suggest that a BCR is like a tweet (or a short post formerly known as a tweet), and like a tweet it only has so many characters or words. Teachers will also make it easier for themselves to read BCRs by reminding students that they must write legibly. Short, legible responses can be read quickly. Regrettably, as many teachers well know, the opposite is also true.

Correct Academic Responses

As described in Chapter 5, correct academic responses (CARs) are a measure of the number of correct and incorrect responses students give to questions. CARs are often expressed as a percentage, and teachers may want to set a goal for the percentage of CARs their students give. CARs can be gathered by coaches or other observers in a teacher's classroom, often in real time, by putting plusses or minuses under students' names on a seating chart, or by teachers as they watch video recordings of their students.

One modification of CARs that can provide valuable information is to record the level of thinking behind student responses. For example, observers might use Anderson and colleagues' (2001) revision of Bloom's taxonomy (remember, understand, apply, analyze, evaluate, create). A simpler method might be to distinguish between lower-level response (remember, understand) and higher-level responses (apply, analyze, evaluate, create). One teacher we know simply distinguishes between teacher-pleasing responses (questions the students thought their teacher wanted to hear) and original responses.

ADVANTAGES AND DISADVANTAGES

In the rush and excitement of guiding a class of students, teachers can lose sight of how students are responding to questions. CARs provide a measure of how well students can recall knowledge, and teachers can find it enlightening to see this kind of data. However, it takes a long time to gather CARs. Also, CARs only provide information on the students who are responding to questions, revealing nothing about the students who do not respond. For this reason, there can be great value in recording which students do and do not respond to questions, perhaps on a seating chart.

Checks for Understanding

Selected-response and brief constructed response tests and quizzes can be used for setting achievement goals or for formative assessment, but they may take too much time to create, complete, and grade if they are going to be used frequently in the classroom. Some teachers use checks for understanding to gather data on student achievement instead. Checks for understanding are simple procedures teachers employ to gather data on each student's learning level or attitude during or at the end of a lesson. They are easy to use, effective, and popular ways to gather data about what students are learning.

Math teachers using checks for understanding, for example, might prompt students to solve their problems on white boards during lessons and then ask students to hold up their white boards so that they can see how well students are performing. Teachers in science classes might ask students to hold up red, yellow, or green cards in answer to questions so that they can see immediately how all students answer questions.

Jim has written about checks for understanding in a several publications: *High-Impact Instruction* (Knight, 2013), *The Impact Cycle* (Knight, 2018), and *The Definitive Guide to Instructional Coaching* (Knight, 2022). Some of the checks for understanding he's described include the following.

EXIT TICKETS

Exit tickets are short notes students hand in at the end of class. Exit tickets are usually completed on small pieces of paper or index cards and may include a writing assignment, a short quiz, or a single question.

WHITE BOARDS

White boards are glossy surfaces that students can use to record non-permanent markings. In many schools, every student is given a small white board to use during class. When teachers have students use white boards, they ask all students to answer a question on their individual white boards and then to hold them up at the same time. Teachers can then lead a clarifying discussion if there are conflicting answers.

RESPONSE CARDS

Response cards include index cards with a yes on one side and a no on the other side, or individual cards with the colors red, yellow, and green on them. When teachers prompt students to use response cards during lessons, they ask students to answer a question by holding up the appropriate card for their answer. As with many other forms of checks for understanding, all students respond at the same time.

CLICKERS AND OTHER ELECTRONIC CHECKS FOR UNDERSTANDING

Various companies sell electronic devices that enable students to respond to questions and send their responses directly to a teacher's computer or tablet. Using such tools, teachers can see immediately which students answered correctly and incorrectly, and tallies of answers can be displayed via a projector or smart board. Increasingly, students use tablets or other digital devices as clickers. These have the advantage of automatically providing data for teachers to analyze. Also, clickers are private communications between teachers and students so students don't have to share their responses in front of their classmates.

THUMBS UP, THUMBS DOWN, THUMBS WIGGLY

With this kind of check for understanding, teachers ask students to communicate their response to questions using their thumbs. Thumbs up means they understand/agree, thumbs down means they don't understand/agree, and holding thumbs horizontally and wiggling means they're not sure if they understand/agree. This kind of check for understanding has the advantages of being inexpensive and portable—teachers can ask students to use their thumbs anywhere, inside or outside the classroom.

TURN-TO-YOUR-NEIGHBOR

After students complete a learning task, teachers can ask them to compare their answer or idea with a neighboring student to see if they have the same answer. If yes, students give the teacher a thumbs up. If no, students give the teacher a thumbs down. When students have different answers, teachers can explore or clarify answers during classroom discussion or individual conferences.

HOT POTATO

This can be a fun way for students to share their knowledge. Hot potato begins with the teacher asking a student a question that tests their understanding of content. If the student gets the answer right, they get to ask a question of another student, testing that student's understanding. The student asking the question must know the answer so they can comment on whether or not the new student gets the correct answer. Teachers can structure this activity in various ways. For example, the teacher or students can pick who will answer the question, and the teacher or students can choose the question. Teachers can also use the 4Rs method Jim described in *High-Impact Instruction* (Knight, 2013) by repeating, rephrasing, or reducing a question, or by offering students a chance to reach out to others in class for help answering.

SOCCER, HOCKEY, BASKETBALL

For this check for understanding, teachers draw a playing field on the white or smart board, and then organize the class into two teams. To start the game, a puck or ball is drawn at the center of the field the teacher has drawn. Then, the teacher asks a question of one team, and if that team gets a correct answer, the teacher moves the ball or puck closer to the other team's goal. If a member of a team gets an answer wrong, the teacher moves the ball or puck toward their own goal. If the ball or puck gets in one team's scoring zone, and they get a wrong answer, or the other team gets a right answer, a goal or basket is scored. The puck or ball is then placed at the center of the field for the restart.

GRAPHIC ORGANIZERS

Asking students to create graphic organizers, such as descriptive, sequential, problem-solution, and compare-and-contrast organizers, is a good check of student understanding. In most cases, students will need to understand the content to be able to create correct graphic organizers.

GAME SHOWS

With a little effort, teachers can develop their own version of popular game shows such as Jeopardy. Teachers should divide the class into teams and give each team review time prior to the game.

JIGSAW GALLERY WALK

Using this format, students are organized into groups and asked to create a poster on chart paper that they can display in the room. The poster should demonstrate the students' knowledge of content covered; for example, a poster might consist of a few bullet points, a picture, a metaphor, or a graphic organizer. Once the groups have finished, students are mixed up so that a new group is formed that includes a member from each initial group. The groups then walk around the room, stopping at each poster. Whoever created the poster explains it to the rest of their new group.

FOUR CORNERS

The teacher gives students a question and asks them to move to a corner of the room based on their answer. For example, a teacher might pose a multiple-choice question and designate each corner of the room as *a*, *b*, *c*, or *d*. Although this type of check for understanding provides limited responses, the formative nature of the assessment allows students to ask clarifying questions, revise answers after the discussion, or face the same question again to reconsider.

QUIZZES OR TESTS

Multiple-choice, true-or-false, fill-in-the-blank, and short-answer quizzes and tests can be used with many of the above assessment tools.

PARAPHRASING

Teachers can assess student understanding by asking students to retell in their own words what they have learned, using words other than those they heard or read when they learned whatever is being learned.

GROUP ANSWERS

Teachers use this strategy to check student understanding by putting students in groups and giving them a task to complete, a question to answer, a term to memorize, or some other assignment. The teacher explains to students that in groups everyone is responsible for everyone's learning and that they'll check with one group member—but they don't know who—to check that everyone has learned what needs to be learned. Thus, all students must ensure that everyone knows whatever is being learned.

WRITING

Students' understanding can also be assessed using numerous writing assessments. Students can be prompted to write a response to a passage they've read, answer a question with a few sentences, write a letter to an author, write a letter of complaint, write a short story to illustrate a concept that has been learned, and so forth. A variation of think, pair, share that we like is write, pair, share. This check for understanding allows students time to respond and gives teachers a permanent product to assess learning.

ADVANTAGES AND DISADVANTAGES

Checks for understanding are easy to use, and they give teachers a quick, clear picture of how well each student is learning what is being taught. However, like selected-response assessments, checks for understanding are less effective at assessing skills and big ideas. Asking a student to hold up a green card if they know how to find the main idea in a paragraph only reveals what students think they can do (or what they think the teacher wants them to report); the green card doesn't tell the teacher if the student can actually do it.

We suggest using signals when you use checks for understanding. For example, a teacher tells students that she is going to count down "3, 2, 1, go" and that when she says "go," she wants all students to respond at the same time. The teacher might even use a hand signal and bring her hand down when she says "go" to prompt students to respond at exactly the same time.

Signals like this have many advantages. They keep students from checking to see how their classmates are responding before they respond. They also allow processing time for students, and as teachers get to know their students, they will better understand how much processing time particular students need.

Rubrics

Tests, quizzes, and checks for understanding can be used effectively and efficiently to assess knowledge, but they are less effective for assessing skills. Asking a student to give you a thumbs up on their ability to give a presentation, for example, isn't as effective as actually watching that student give a presentation and assessing their performance using a rubric. Rubrics are also well known for bringing objectivity to subjective learning situations; for example, when grading a persuasive essay or judging the quality of rhetoric during a debate. For that reason, we suggest educators use rubrics to assess skills.

In their *Introduction to Rubrics* (2005), Dannelle Stevens and Antonia Levi define a rubric as follows:

> At its most basic, a rubric is a scoring tool that lays out the specific expectations for an assignment. Rubrics divide an assignment into its component parts and provide a detailed description of what constitutes acceptable or unacceptable levels of performance for each of those parts (p. 3).

CHECKLISTS

Checklists, according to Susan Brookhart (2013), are not actually rubrics, because they "lack descriptions of performance quality" (p. 76), one of two defining characteristics of rubrics—the other being "criteria for students' work" (p. 76). However, she adds that checklists are "in the family of rubrics" (p. 76). Checklists are effective tools for assessing something simple or discrete enough so that it can be assessed with a yes or no answer. Thus, checklists are excellent for assessing whether or not students have completed some part of an assignment or some part of a process. If one item on a checklist is "Begin your paragraph with a topic sentence," that line just assesses whether or not a topic sentence is included in the paragraph. It's not an assessment of the quality of the topic sentence.

CHECKLIST: THE WRITING PROCESS

Did I ...	
Use strategies (such as clustering, free writing, brainstorming) to get ideas out of my head?	
Use strategies (such as planning maps, the frame, orderly notes) to organize my ideas?	
Write about a topic that I care about?	
Shape my writing to speak to a particular audience?	
Use editing strategies (such as COPS, non-translatable language, Twitter test, active voice, shorter is better) to make my writing clearer?	
Did my writing express my chosen voice? Chosen point of view (POV)?	
Address categories of error that arose in the previous day's work?	

Source: From *The Definitive Guide to Instructional Coaching* by Jim Knight, 2021.

SINGLE-POINT RUBRICS (SPRS)

Jennifer Gonzalez, who writes the blog *Cult of Pedagogy* (https://www.cultofpedagogy.com/), has popularized the use of single-point rubrics. This form of assessment includes a single criterion at the center of the rubric, with space on either side for someone (teacher, student, or peer) to add comments related to areas for improvement and evidence of exceeding standards. Gonzalez lists three advantages of these simple rubrics:

» Teachers find them easier and faster to create.

» Students find them easier to read when preparing an assignment.

» They allow for higher-quality feedback because teachers must specify key problem areas and notable areas of excellence for a particular student rather than choosing from a list of generic descriptions.

(https://www.cultofpedagogy.com/single-point-rubric/)

SINGLE-POINT RUBRIC: THE WRITING PROCESS

Areas for Improvement	Criteria	Strengths
	Planning Addresses all elements of the prompt	
	Revising Uses appropriate vocabulary throughout	
	Editing Conforms to conventions of standard English	
	Rewriting Uses transitions appropriately	
	New Approaches Allow students to experiment with writing in different ways	

Source: From *The Definitive Guide to Instructional Coaching* by Jim Knight, 2021.

ANALYTIC RUBRICS (MULTIPLE-POINT RUBRICS)

Another option for assessing skills is the analytic rubric, which provides more comprehensive descriptions of different levels of accomplishment or performance. Multiple-point rubrics usually sort each criterion of a rubric into different levels with words such as *beginning, developing, accomplished,* or *exemplary.* Effective multiple-point rubrics provide a rich description of success criteria for any learning process or product.

EXAMPLE ANALYTIC RUBRIC

Score	4	3	2	1	0
Planning	Addresses all the elements of the prompt. Clearly demonstrates attention to task and purpose and chooses evidence, organization, level of language, and writing style according to that task and purpose. Clearly demonstrates attention to audience and chooses evidence, organization, level of language, and writing style according to the needs of that audience.	Addresses most elements of the prompt. Mostly demonstrates attention to task and purpose and chooses most evidence, organization, level of language, and writing style according to that task and purpose. Mostly demonstrates attention to audience and chooses most evidence, organization, level of language, and writing style according to the needs of that audience.	Addresses some elements of the prompt. Demonstrates some attention to task and purpose and chooses some evidence, organization, level of language, and writing style according to that task and purpose. Demonstrates some attention to audience and chooses some evidence, organization, level of language, and writing style according to the needs of that audience.	Addresses the prompt minimally if at all. Demonstrates little to no attention to task and purpose and does not appear to choose evidence, organization, level of language, and writing style according to that task and purpose. Demonstrates little to no attention to audience and does not appear to choose evidence, organization, level of language, and writing style according to the needs of that audience.	There is no response, or the response is inappropriate.
Revising	Consistently uses appropriate grade-level academic and general vocabulary throughout the piece. Consistently maintains purpose and focus throughout the piece.	Uses mostly appropriate grade-level academic and general vocabulary throughout the piece. Mostly maintains purpose and focus throughout the piece.	Uses some appropriate grade-level academic and general vocabulary throughout the piece. Demonstrates some purpose and focus throughout the piece.	Uses little to no appropriate grade-level academic and general vocabulary throughout the piece. Maintains little to no purpose and focus throughout the piece.	There is no response, or the response is inappropriate.
Editing	Consistently conforms to the conventions of standard written English. Language and syntax are consistently clear and coherent.	Mostly conforms to the conventions of standard written English. Language and syntax are mostly clear and coherent.	Sometimes conforms to the conventions of standard written English. Language and syntax are sometimes clear and coherent.	Does not conform to the conventions of standard written English. Language and syntax are not clear and coherent.	There is no response, or the response is inappropriate.

Source: Rubric created by ICG consultant Sharon Thomas.

ADVANTAGES AND DISADVANTAGES

Rubrics are a highly effective way to assess products and performances. We prefer single-point rubrics, when appropriate, because they are easier to understand and grade. However, the downside of rubrics, especially analytic rubrics, is that they take a significant amount of time to create and use for grading. One way to address this issue is to teach students how to self-assess and peer-assess their work. An added benefit of self-assessment is that it is an essential part of learning how to learn.

 PRO TIP

When teachers come together to create rubrics, they can learn a great deal from each other, thereby improving the quality of the rubrics they create. One thing to keep in mind is that rubrics are primarily for students, so they should be written in non-translatable language that students easily understand. The language in rubrics should be correct, accurate, and as simple as possible.

Interviews

A final method of assessing student learning is interviews, also discussed in Chapter 5. Interviews provide a sample of the perspectives of various students toward their experiences in a classroom. We suggest coaches or teachers interview at least 20% of the students in a class to get a deeper insight into what students are and are not learning and how well students can make connections and transfer what they are learning.

Interviews can be conducted by instructional coaches, with the coaches sharing the results with the collaborating teacher once interviews are completed, or they can be conducted by the teacher, with the coach teaching the lesson to free up the teacher. While students may be more forthcoming if they are talking to the coach since the coach isn't assessing them, teachers may be able to ask probing questions that help them better understand where students are succeeding and struggling. One-to-one conversations can also deepen the relationships between teachers and students.

In each situation, coaches and teachers need to create questions that are most useful for a particular class. They also need to consider what length of interview would yield the most useful information. A longer interview leads to more in-depth information, but a shorter interview allows time for more students to be interviewed.

ADVANTAGES AND DISADVANTAGES

Interviews allow educators to gain a rich understanding of what students are learning, how they are learning, and where they are experiencing roadblocks. The major challenge with interviews is that they take a lot of time, and they only provide a sample of students' experiences—the 20% sample discussed above. If you want to gather data weekly, that requires a huge time commitment for a coach or a coach and teacher. Consequently, you may find that interviews with a combination of other measures is necessary to supplement your growing understanding of student progress.

 PRO TIP

If we want students to share helpful information during interviews, we need to ensure that they feel safe. For this reason, interviewers want to make it very clear to students at the start of the interview that what students say has no impact on their grades and that the interviews are intended to help the teacher create better learning for everyone. Also, no matter what students say, they need to be thanked for their comments, and interviewers need to refrain from any kind of comment that might be seen as defensive or confrontational. Students need to feel that their comments, whatever their form, are welcome and helpful. One advantage of coaches doing the interviews is that they can assure students that their comments are confidential.

How to Ensure the Assessment Is Appropriate

We've discussed six different ways to gather data. All of them can be used to assess different levels and kinds of learning, but not all levels and kinds of learning can be assessed by every assessment. Educators need to consider carefully whether they are assessing knowledge, skills, or big ideas and whether they're assessing acquisition, connection, or transfer of that knowledge, and then they must choose the most appropriate tool accordingly.

We created the table below to help educators identify which assessment is best for the kind and level of learning they intend to assess. As always, the Data Rules apply to the choice of assessment tool. That is, effective assessments should foster hope, be tied to professional learning, be easy to use, objective, valid, and frequently gathered. Ideally, assessments better support professional learning when they are chosen and gathered by teachers.

As the table indicates, some assessments serve more purposes than others. What the table doesn't show, however, is which assessments are easier to use. For example, BCRs may not be highly effective for all levels and kinds of learning, but their ease of use means that they are very popular.

The form we've created is not carved in stone. We have no doubt that there are innovative ways to use checks for understanding, for example, to assess big ideas. The table is simply a guideline you can use to support you as you consider how best to gather data on the level and kind of learning you plan to assess.

CHOOSING THE RIGHT ASSESSMENT

K = Knowledge   S = Skill   B = Big Ideas

Assessment	Acquisition	Connection	Transfer
Selected Response	K		
Checks for Understanding	K	K	K
Brief Constructed Response	K S B	K S B	K S B
Correct Academic Responses	K B	K	

Assessment	Acquisition	Connection	Transfer
Single-Point Rubric	K S B	K S B	K S B
Analytic Rubric	K S B	K S B	K S B
Interviews	K S B	K S B	K S B

To Sum Up

As pointed out in this chapter, preparing to gather data related to achievement involves two steps. First, identify what you want students to learn. Second, determine how you will assess that learning.

To identify what students will learn, we suggest educators:

» Create guiding questions, which are questions that guide teachers as they determine the knowledge, skills, and big ideas they want students to learn during a unit; and

» Create specific proficiencies for each guiding question. Specific proficiencies are sentences that precisely state the knowledge, skills, and big ideas students need to learn, usually a distinct component of student learning (such as a fact, skill, or principle) that can and likely should be assessed individually.

To assess what students have learned, we suggest educators:

» Use tests, quizzes, and checks for understanding to gather data on what students have learned; and

» Use assessment tools from the family of rubrics, including checklists, single-point rubrics, and multi-point (analytic) rubrics.

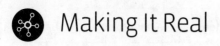

Making It Real

Students

In many learning situations, students can provide meaningful input into how their learning will be assessed. For example, in *Student-Involved Formative Assessment* (2005), Rick Stiggins suggests teachers share a variety of writing samples with students and ask them to identify the strengths and weaknesses of the writing. Then, student comments can be used to create the learning assessment. When students are involved in creating their assessments, they will understand their success criteria better and be more committed to creating quality work.

Teachers

The work of creating guiding questions and specific proficiencies should be done by those whose teaching will be built around those important instructional elements. When all the teachers who teach a particular course are brought together to create curriculum, teachers' content knowledge increases significantly. In *Unmistakable Impact* (Knight, 2011), Jim describes a process, intensive-learning teams, that ensures that everyone who teaches a course has a voice in how that course will be organized.

Coaches

In the best situations, teachers can come together to collaborate and develop curriculum in a process such as intensive-learning teams mentioned above. In effectively organized collaborative learning, teachers with different knowledge learn with and from each other, gaining deeper understanding of content they teach.

In some settings, however, a community learning process like intensive-learning teams isn't possible. In such situations, coaches can collaborate with teachers to create questions, proficiencies, and assessments. This is intensive work, so it is helpful to teachers if they can have a half-day of release time to collaborate with their coach.

Administrators

Leaders can encourage curriculum development by proposing a vision for the curriculum and then supporting educators as they create that curriculum. Each administrator will want to articulate a vision that is right for their setting, but that vision will likely be an adaptation of the idea that "all students know how well their learning is progressing, and teachers, too, know how well all students are learning."

Administrators can support curriculum development by providing opportunities for teachers and administrators to get together to develop guiding questions, specific proficiencies, learning maps, and assessments for entire courses. When such collaboration is going on, it is important that an administrator is present in the meeting to say yes or no to particular plans teachers are creating. Teachers' enthusiasm for curriculum development will take a serious hit if they invest a lot of effort in creating questions, proficiencies, and assessments, only to be told by an administrator that their plans need to be changed.

 # Going Deeper

The information in this chapter is possible only because of the work of many other authors. Our ideas about guiding questions were influenced, in particular, by the work of Keith Lenz, the primary author of several helpful texts, including *The Course Organizer Routine* (1998), *The Unit Organizer Routine* (1994), and *The Lesson Organizer Routine* (1993). Additionally, our thinking about guiding questions, like many educators around the world, was influenced by Jay McTighe and Grant Wiggins's *Understanding by Design* (2005) and Larry Ainsworth and Kira Donovan's *Rigorous Curriculum Design* (2019). Our writing about specific proficiencies was influenced by Rick Stiggins's discussion of propositions in *Student-Involved Assessment for Learning* (2004).

When it comes to assessment, our writing on checks for understanding was influenced by Doug Fisher and Nancy Frey's *Checking for Understanding* (2014). Danelle Stevens and Antonia Levi's *Introduction to Rubrics* (2005) and Susan Brookhart's *How to Create and Use Rubrics for Formative Assessment and Grading* (2013) were both invaluable resources for building our understanding of effective rubrics.

Learning That Transfers (2021), by Julie Stern, Krista Ferraro, Kayla Duncan, and Trevor Aleo, significantly influenced our understanding of conceptual understanding and the acquisition, connect, and transfer elements of the ACT model. Finally, we also recommend Dylan Wiliam and Siobahán Leahy's *Embedded Formative Assessment* (2015) and Jan Chappuis's *Seven Strategies of Assessment for Learning* (2014).

RESEARCH ON ASSESSMENT DATA

Scan for more on research related to different forms of assessment data profiled in this chapter.

TEACHING

is about

seeing teaching practices
that affect students' learning
and well-being

*enhanced or
diminished by*

*fostered
through*

*revealed
in*

Interactions

Questions

Student
and Teacher
Talk

- Ratio of interaction
- Corrections
- Interaction analytic
- Power with and
  power over

- Kind
- Type
- Level
- Number

CHAPTER 7

TEACHING

The goal of all teacher professional development and evaluation should be to foster improvement in teaching that fosters improvement in student learning and well-being. For that reason, we need to gather data on teaching. This chapter provides an overview of data on teaching, organized into three categories: interactions, questions, and talk. You can skip this chapter if you're sure you're gathering the highest-impact data as part of your coaching or evaluation. You should read it if you want to learn more about data that reveal the impact of teaching and describe your interactions with students.

CHAPTER RESOURCES

Access charts, diagrams, research, and resources from this chapter.

One child, one teacher, one book, one pen can change the world.

MALALA YOUSAFZAI

Wendy Reinke is a University of Missouri researcher studying positive behavior. Years ago, she led a study looking at the power of sharing data with teachers. Reinke measured two kinds of data: (a) the number of times students were disruptive during a class and (b) how frequently teachers praised students. She wanted to find what impact sharing the data on positive attention would have on students, which was part of her ongoing research on what she refers to as the classroom checkup (Reinke et al., 2011).

The results, as the form on the next page shows, were conclusive. As positive attention went up, disruptions went down. That is, the research revealed that when teachers understand the impact of their actions by seeing data, they will change their actions, and those changes will lead to improved student–teacher interactions and ultimately greater student success.

What Dr. Reinke did in her research—gathering data on two things at once—is often what instructional coaches or other observers have to do when gathering data related to instructional improvement. On the one hand, they need to record data related to a student-focused goal, such as time on task, educator response data, interruptions, level of student responses, and so on. On the other hand, they need to gather data on what teachers do. The teacher data usually aren't the goal for coaching—what matters is an unmistakably positive change in student learning or well-being. However, teacher data need to be gathered so teachers can see that what they do often has an impact on what their students do. In short, gathering data on teaching helps us get clearer on what is working, what isn't working, and what should be reinforced or changed.

IMPACT OF POSITIVE ATTENTION DATA ON STUDENTS

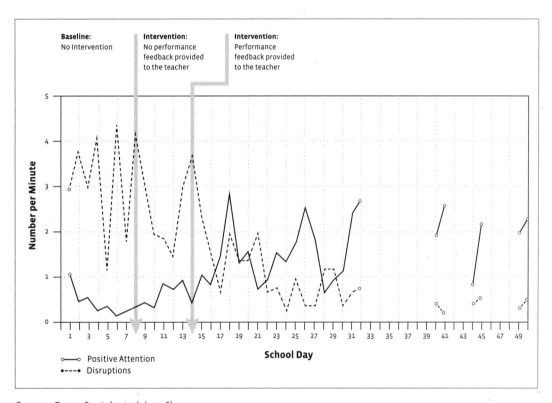

Source: From Sprick et al. (2006).

The Data Rules apply to gathering data on teaching just as they apply to data on student engagement or achievement. Data have to be gathered frequently, reliably, validly, objectively, hopefully, and ideally chosen by and gathered by the teacher, often using video. Some of the teaching behaviors on which data are most frequently gathered are described in the following.

Forms of Data Frequently Gathered on Teaching Behavior

____

Ratio of Interaction

Wendy Reinke was gathering data on praise, one aspect of a kind of data known as ratio of interaction. Ratio of interaction measures how often teachers give attention to students when those students are acting in ways that promote learning compared with how often teachers give attention to students who are acting in ways that don't promote learning (some might refer to this as off-task, or more commonly misbehaving). If teachers give the bulk of their attention to inappropriate behavior, ironically, their attempts to eliminate bad behavior by correcting it can actually increase that behavior. A student might think, "If I do what I'm supposed to do, I'm invisible, but if I act up, I get the teacher's attention every time."

A simple analogy illustrates why ratio-of-interaction data are so helpful. Imagine a plant sitting on a windowsill facing the sun. In most situations, if the plant isn't moved, its leaves slowly begin to turn toward the sunlight. The whole plant will turn to the window to soak up sunlight.

In the classroom a teacher's attention is like sunlight, and students will adjust their behavior in order to get their teacher's attention in the same way the plant in the window turns toward the sun. Positive behavior expert Randy Sprick likes to say that every time a teacher gives attention to a student, it is similar to the teacher giving that student a five-dollar bill. The question then is "When you give students your attention, what behavior are you rewarding them for?"

Often, the answer is that students are getting our attention for misbehaving. Our brains are wired to see what isn't working more easily that what is working—look at a class with 27 students on task and one student off task, and who do you see?—so we often find ourselves giving our attention to students who are acting unproductively more than to students who are acting productively.

As far as we know, there is no ideal ratio of positive attention to negative attention. Relationship researcher John Gottman (2001) has found that for healthy relationships there should be at least a 5-to-1 ratio of positive to negative attention. Psychologist Barbara Frederickson (2009), on the other hand, has found that there should be at least a 3-to-1 ratio of attention to ensure healthy teams and relationships. Regardless of the number, what matters is that the teacher gives a lot more attention to positive student behavior than negative student behavior because negative interactions usually have much more staying power than positive interactions. Simply put, teachers should give enough positive attention to students so that students can clearly see that the best way to get their teacher's attention is to act in ways that promote learning for themselves and others—acting productively.

Ratio of interaction assesses how teachers communicate to all students that each of them matters. A positive ratio of interaction tells students that their teacher sees and values them and thinks that what they say is important. This kind of data also helps teachers see whether they are interacting equitably by giving all students the same amount and quality of attention.

The easiest way to gather data on ratio of interaction, as we have seen for other forms of data, is to record the data on the collaborating teacher's seating chart. When a teacher attends to a student for a positive reason, you put a plus sign on the chart under that student's name. When the teacher attends to students for a negative reason, you put a minus sign under their name. When the teacher makes a positive statement to the entire class—"you guys are coming up with some great ideas today"—or a negative statement—"everybody be quiet"—you can put a plus or minus on the side of the chart. While common, it is important to remember that the impact of group feedback is often defused across the group and, while felt by students, is less impactful in comparison to individual interaction.

RATIO OF INTERACTION FORM

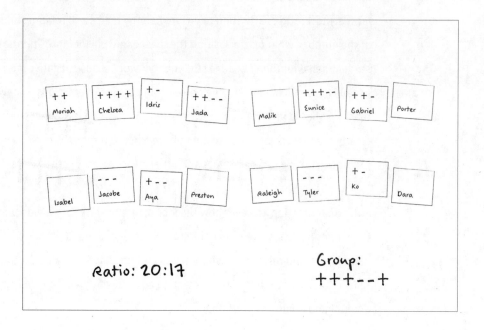

The power of using the seating chart in this way is that teachers can immediately see which students are getting the most or least attention for positive or negative behaviors just by looking at the chart. In some cases, the data may also help teachers become of aware of implicit biases by showing which students are getting only one kind of attention or no attention. If the teacher interacts with male students twice as often as female students, or interacts with BIPOC (black, indigenous, people of color) students differently than other students, for example, the teacher may realize that they need to think deeply about how they see and support all students.

Of course, a seating chart won't work for classes where students are not sitting at desks, so when this is the case, we suggest coaches simply keep a tally of plusses and minuses to share with teachers after class, as shown in the form below.

MEASURING RATIO OF INTERACTIONS, WITHOUT A SEATING CHART

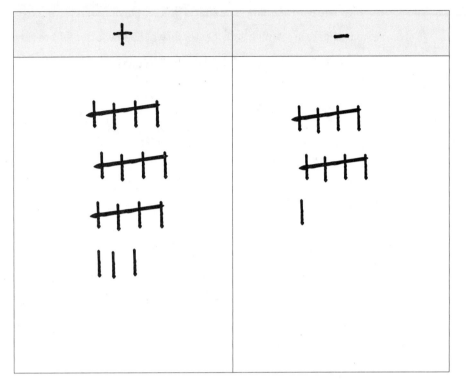

Corrections

Continuing with our botanical analogies, when you plant a garden, you need to pull the weeds. If you put some seeds in the ground, water and fertilize your plants but ignore the weeds, eventually the weeds will spread and take over the whole garden, choking out the seedlings you planted. If you want your flowers to grow, you have to pull the weeds.

Much the same thing can be said for the classroom. If teachers want to create a positive learning environment for students, they need to correct behavior that interferes with learning. Let's be clear: corrections should not be used to put students down—see the discussion of power below. Corrections should be used to create the safest possible learning environment for students. If you don't correct students, there is a great risk that negative behavior, just like the weeds in the garden, will take over the class, thereby decreasing psychological safety and, eventually, learning.

Before data on corrections are gathered, teachers need to clarify in their own mind what behaviors need to be corrected. They can do this by listing (a) what behaviors interfere with learning (side conversations, playing with technology, refusing to participate in learning activities) or (b) what behaviors interfere with psychological safety (insulting fellow students, vulgar language, micro-aggressions). Different teachers will inevitably identify different behaviors that need to be corrected depending on their beliefs about teaching and learning and depending on their students. Tight structures for learning might be essential in some classrooms and unnecessary or even intrusive in others.

Once teachers have listed the behaviors that are unacceptable to them, they need to identify how they will correct those behaviors the first, second, third, and (we hope not too often) the fourth time they see them. For example, a teacher who wants to stop students from using technology in class might make a list like this. First time: eye contact; second time: proximity; third time: verbal warning; fourth time: extra assignment to make up for lost time.

Clearly communicating what is not acceptable in a classroom creates a safer, better learning environment for all students. As Brené Brown has said, "clear is kind" (2018, p. 47). However, we must resist the temptation to implement our corrections robotically, ignoring the emotions and true needs of our students. Therefore, we should always be asking, "What is the root cause of this behavior?"

To gather data on corrections, we suggest using a form such as the one included below. Observers can use the form while watching teachers teach, and teachers can use the form while watching video of their class. On the form, list the kinds of behavior the teacher wants to correct in the "behavior to be corrected" column; then put a tally in the "observed" column whenever you see a student doing the identified behavior and a tally in the "corrected" column whenever the behavior is corrected. The goal is for the teacher to consistently correct behavior when it occurs so that the observed and corrected columns have the same number. When expectations are clear, and students receive consistent and frequent positive attention for learning behaviors, the number in both columns should consistently go down.

CORRECTIONS FORM

Behavior to Be Corrected	Observed	Corrected

Interaction Analysis

All data have limitations. Ratio-of-interaction and corrections data provide snap-shots of what happens in a classroom, but they do not capture the depth or impact of different interactions. For example, some people can describe an interaction they had with a teacher who truly inspired them to make a giant leap forward. Others can point to comments that hit them hard in a negative way. When we gather data on ratio of interaction, a life-changing positive comment by a teacher is given the same weight as a one-time thumbs up. How can we go deeper?

One way to gather deeper (though less quantifiable) data is to analyze each inter-action between teachers and students. We refer to this kind of data gathering as—no surprise here—interaction analysis. To gather this kind of data, coaches need to record the name of each student and, as briefly as possible, the nature of the interaction between the teacher and the student. For group interactions, the coach can simply write down the word "group" and then note what was said or done.

After the observer has gathered the data, the observer and teacher (or the teacher on their own) can sit down and review the data. We find it especially helpful to look for patterns in the data. Are there particular students who are getting most of the teacher's attention? Is the teacher over- or under-responding to anything students do or say? Teachers might also find it enlightening to code their interactions as ones that foster (a) belonging or (b) alienation, bearing in mind Gottman's (2001) finding that a minimum ratio of interaction for a healthy relationship is 5 to 1.

INTERACTION ANALYSIS

Student	Interaction What was said, done, communicated nonverbally or otherwise	−	+

Power With and Power Over

One final distinction relates to the interactions between teachers and students. In *High-Impact Instruction* (Knight, 2013), Jim wrote about the difference between "power over" and "power with." Power over, he wrote, occurs when "teachers use power to dominate, often simply because the feeling of domination is intoxicating … power over students can be detrimental to everyone in the classroom, including the teacher" (p. 264).

"Power over" is manifested in psychological bullying, where teachers believe that there is only one right way—their way—and that pupils are beneath them. In the worst circumstances, pupils feel powerless when a teacher dominates them. However, "power over … is not always as obvious as psychological bullying. It can surface when teachers subtly ridicule a student in front of her peers, when they lecture students to show who is boss, when they glare at a student who is out of line, and when they use their much greater knowledge and experience to show up a student in an in-class debate" (Knight, 2013, pp. 264-265). In contrast, "power with" involves real power created with students. "Teachers taking the 'power with' approach practice empathizing with, connecting with, and respecting students" (p. 267).

The simplest way for teachers to determine how they use power in their classrooms is to watch video of their lessons and look for specific behaviors that communicate power with or power over. Most likely, everyone will interpret power differently. We suggest that power with is usually occurring when we give students our full attention, affirm students, refrain from interrupting students, avoid micro-aggressions, make bids for connection with students, and communicate the same degree of respect to all students. Teachers who want to reflect on how they use power can use the checklist below to analyze their interactions.

 ## CHECKLIST: POWER WITH

When teaching, did you …	✓
Give students your full attention when they were talking?	
Affirm students for their contribution (either verbally or nonverbally)?	
Refrain from interrupting students when they were talking?	

When teaching, did you ...	
Avoid micro-aggressions such as sarcasm, singling students out, power-tripping, and other actions that communicate a lack of respect?	
Make bids for connection and appropriately turn toward students' bids for connection?	
Communicate the same degree of respect to all students?	
Address categories of error that arose in the previous day's work?	

Questions

Another kind of interaction, of course, is the use of questions. Questions are such a big part of instruction that we include them as a separate form of data. Studies suggest that teachers, on average, ask questions about 20% of the time (Hattie, 2008).

When teachers consider what questions to ask, one of their first thoughts should be what kind of learning the question supports. Jim has written about learning as being either "closed" or "open" (Knight, 2021, p. 219). With closed learning, the teacher's goal is that students will understand content exactly as it is taught. That is, the picture in the students' minds will be the same as the picture in the teacher's mind. For example, when teaching students how to appreciate poetry, the teacher may want students to understand that the literary term "alliteration" is defined as "the repetition of the same sounds—usually initial consonants of words or of stressed syllables—in any sequence of neighbouring words" (Baldick, p. 89). That shared understanding, that same picture in the students' and teacher's minds, is important because it means that, in this case, students can consistently and clearly talk about alliteration with others.

With open learning, on the other hand, the teacher's goal is to create an opportunity for students to construct their own understanding of whatever is being learned. Thus, the same teacher teaching students how to appreciate poetry might share Mary Oliver's poem "The Summer Day."

Then, providing an opportunity for students to apply the poem to their own life, she might ask students, "What do you think of the way the poet is using her 'wild and precious life' in this poem?" Then, she might ask students to write down some thoughts about how they want to live their lives and ask students to share their thoughts. In this example of open learning, the teacher's goal is to create a learning experience where students construct their own understanding of what is being learned. That is, in contrast to closed learning, in open learning the goal is that students paint their own picture of what they are learning.

We believe that neither type of learning is superior to the other. Sometimes students need to develop a vocabulary or become proficient in a skill; at other times they need to make their own personal connections to what they are learning. Below we describe how teachers should choose the appropriate question by describing three categories: the kind, type, and level of question.

KIND: OPEN (OR OPEN-ENDED) AND CLOSED (OR CLOSE-ENDED) QUESTIONS

Most educators feel comfortable talking about open and closed questions. However, a quick internet search reveals that there are actually different definitions for these terms. Most people state that open questions produce longer responses, whereas closed questions produce shorter responses. We would add that open questions have an unlimited number of responses—"What do you like about the Star Wars movies?"—and closed questions have a limited number of answers, often a very small number like one, two, or three—"Who played Chewbacca in the Star Wars films?" [Peter Mayhew].

Open questions are usually more effective for generating open learning because their unlimited nature leaves room for students to make thoughtful, expansive responses. Closed questions are often more effective for closed learning where the teachers likely will need to assess whether or not students' learning is correct.

TYPE: RIGHT OR WRONG VS. OPINION

A second kind of data to gather related to questions is right-or-wrong vs. opinion questions. Right-or-wrong questions have either a correct or an incorrect answer: "In what year was the first Star Wars film released in the United States?" [1977]. The answer to a right-or-wrong question isn't up for debate. The answer is always either correct or incorrect. These types of questions are very important for confirming how well students understand what's been taught. Often right-or-wrong questions are closed questions, but not always.

Opinion questions, in contrast, do not have correct or incorrect answers. Opinion questions ask students for their perspective on a topic, not for a right or a wrong answer. Often, opinion questions are open questions, but not always. Teachers can also ask closed opinion questions; that is, questions that students can't get wrong, but to which there is a limited number of responses: "Which is your favorite Star Wars movie?" Opinion questions can also still be grounded in a text so that students provide evidence to support their opinions. Teachers might ask, "Is Han Solo a hero or anti-hero in the movie *A New Hope*? Provide examples to justify your opinion."

The distinction between right-or-wrong and opinion questions is important when it comes to classroom discussions. We have often worked with teachers who are frustrated because they ask questions but students are reluctant to respond. This is a wonderful opportunity for reflection about what else might be happening in the learning environment. Anyone, children or adults, can be hesitant to answer a right-or-wrong question unless they are in safe situations where a lot of right-or-wrong questions are being asked, such as during effective direct instruction. Therefore, if teachers want a lively discussion about a topic in class, their students will be more likely to respond to opinion questions (which they can't get wrong) than to right-or-wrong questions.

LEVEL: KNOWLEDGE, SKILLS, BIG IDEAS

As we mentioned in Chapters 5 and 6, there are many different frameworks for describing level of questions. Most educational organizations have adopted some way of looking at levels of questions, be it old Bloom (Bloom et al., 1956), new Bloom (Anderson et al., 2001), Costa's *Levels of Thinking* (Costa, 1985), DOK (Francis, 2021), SOLO (Biggs & Collis, 1982), or something else. When educators are gathering data on levels of questions, we suggest they just choose their district's method.

We have found, however, that many teachers find the levels of questions to be confusing and end up spending a lot of time trying to figure out the different levels.

One useful simplification is provided by our colleague Keith Lenz (2004), who writes the following:

> We have found in talking to teachers over the years that, in practice, they find the six levels of Bloom's taxonomy cumbersome, and that the levels overlap a great deal. We have reconfigured the taxonomy of cognitive objectives to three levels: acquisition, manipulation, and generalization. Acquisitions correspond to Bloom's levels of knowledge and comprehension; manipulation corresponds to application, analysis, and synthesis; and generalization corresponds to evaluation. (p. 57)

One further simplification is offered by Lynn Erickson in *Concept-Based Curriculum and Instruction for the Thinking Classroom* (2007). She suggests educators consider the knowledge, skills, and big ideas students need to learn. Indeed, she suggests that instruction should involve all three levels of thinking—addressing the knowledge students need to learn, the skills they need to acquire, and the big ideas students need to understand so that they can appreciate the concepts, principles, themes, patterns, and "aha" aspects of learning.

Each organization and educator will need to choose whether they will use the ideas of Bloom, Marzano, Anderson, Lenz, or Erickson, but whatever they choose, chances are that levels of questions will be an important kind of data to gather. In general, we have found that lower-level questions, such as knowledge and skills, are more frequently appropriate for closed learning and that higher-level questions, such as big-idea questions, are more appropriate for opinion questions.

AVERAGE NUMBER OF QUESTIONS ASKED EVERY 10 MINUTES (OPPORTUNITIES TO RESPOND)

One final kind of data to gather related to questions is the number of questions asked by the teacher during a lesson. Often this kind of data is grouped with other kinds of responses (such as turn to your neighbor, thumbs up thumbs down, choral responses, response cards, etc.; see Chapter 6), referred to as opportunities to respond.

Sprick and her colleagues (2021) suggest that there is more student engagement when teachers provide at least four opportunities to respond during direct instruction, which is generally what we mean by closed learning. What matters is not the exact number of questions asked, however, but rather whether students are engaged and learning. If students aren't engaged and learning, educators can experiment with increasing the number of opportunities to respond.

Increasing the number of opportunities to respond may increase engagement and learning during closed learning, where the goal is for students to learn the content in the way that the teacher wants them to learn it. But it isn't advised for open learning, where asking too many questions can interfere with student discussion and higher-order thinking. Once again, educators need to be cautious in their choice of strategy, what works for one form of learning (a high number of opportunities to respond during closed learning) might interfere with learning during another form (open learning).

HOW TO GATHER QUESTION DATA

Fortunately, kind, type, and level of questions are some of the easiest kinds of data to gather. Ideally, teachers should listen to or watch recordings of their lessons and use one of the forms included below to code their questions. If teachers are unable to gather data, coaches can observe a class and gather data using the same forms.

Question data can also be gathered along with student engagement data. For example, observers can gather data on which students respond, how frequently students respond, and the level of their responses. They can also gather time-on-task data, and students can share information about their cognitive or emotional engagement using one of the methods described in Chapter 5.

Video also provides a rich picture of the impact questions can have on learning. As we've mentioned previously, educators who record a lesson to learn about their use of questions may find it helpful to turn their camera toward their students and then watch the video to see how each question affects students. When teachers set student-focused goals related to engagement and they see their students' engagement levels increase as their questions become more effective, it can be highly motivating.

SHORT QUESTION FORM

Start _____   Finish _____

Kind	Type	Level

OTR: _____/_____

Kind: _____   Type: _____   Level: _____

LONG QUESTION FORM

Start _____   Finish _____

Questions	Kind	Type	Level

Teacher Talk vs. Student Talk

When teachers watch video of themselves teaching, they often notice how much they talk and how little their students talk. Many educators agree with the statement that whoever is doing the talking is usually doing the learning (Clinton et al., 2014). We have not found a study that definitively states the ideal ratio for teacher and student talk. Suggestions range from 80% student talk to 30% student talk. We believe the most effective percentage of teacher and student talk will vary depending on the kind of learning that is occurring in a classroom. For example, the percentage of teacher and student talk will likely be different during direct instruction than during small-group learning.

TEACHER TALK VS. STUDENT TALK

See QR code for more information more on research related to teacher talk vs. student talk.

Another working assumption we hold is that in most classrooms, students should talk more. During one recent visit to a high school, we collected data indicating that in the first two-and-one-half hours of our visit across three classrooms, students only spoke three times (and one was a request to use the bathroom!). These teaching data, like all teaching data described in this chapter, could be connected to a student-focused goal for increased achievement or engagement to see what impact, if any, arises from a change in the ratio of teacher and student talk.

Gathering data on teacher and student talk can be a bit complicated because sometimes the teacher is talking, sometimes students are talking, and sometimes students and teacher are talking at the same time. We suggest observers use the form below, but as with all data, we recommend they come up with a decision rule for deciding when they will code teacher talk, student talk, or teacher and student talk.

TEACHER-STUDENT TALK

Start _____   Finish _____

Teacher Talk	Student Talk	Teacher and Student Talk

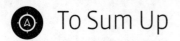

To Sum Up

As described throughout this chapter, gathering teaching data provides a way for educators to see how their teaching practices affect students' engagement and achievement. And just like student engagement data and achievement data, the gathering of teacher data should be guided by the Data Rules. We suggest gathering the following kinds of data:

» Ratio of interaction: How often teachers give attention to students when those students are acting in ways that promote learning compared to how often teachers give attention to students who are acting in ways that don't promote learning.

» Corrections: Assessing the number of correctible behaviors identified by the teachers and the number of times the behavior is corrected by students.

» Interaction analysis: Data gathered for each interaction between teachers and students.

» Power with and power over: Power with involves authentic power teachers develop with students, in contrast to power over, which is coercive power teachers hold over students to keep them in place.

» Questions: Involve choosing the right kind of question for the right kind of learning (open or closed), including:

  • Kind of question (open and closed).

  • Type of question (right-or-wrong vs. opinion questions).

  • Level of question (such as knowledge, skills, big ideas).

  • Average number of questions.

» Teacher talk: Some researchers contend that the more students engage in productive talk, the more they will learn, so it is helpful to gather data on the percentage of a lesson during which the teacher is talking and students are talking.

⬤ Making It Real

Students

One of the easiest and most effective ways for educators to learn about what is and what is not working in a class is to ask the people who are experiencing the class—the students. What we have learned is that students will tell you what they think. Sometimes the greatest barrier to asking students for their feedback is our own timidity about hearing what students have to say. Like most feedback, not all student feedback will be accurate, but all feedback, accurate or inaccurate, can help us improve (Stone & Heen, 2014).

Every teacher will have particular questions they'd like to ask their students about instruction, but as a starting point, some questions might include:

» What's been working in the class?

» What would you like to see more of?

» What would you like to see less of?

» What have you seen other teachers do that you think could improve your experiences in our class?

» What would you like your teacher to know about you that she might not know about you?

» Is there anything else you'd like to share about how we can improve this course for you?

These questions could be given to students as exit tickets—perhaps one question at a time—or used as interview questions that a coach or teacher might ask students to learn more from them. By asking students for their opinion, educators communicate that they value their insights and that they value learning and continuous improvement—two important messages for students to hear. Also, there is a very good chance that students will offer valuable insights and strategies that can make learning more effective.

Teachers

In our experience, teachers find that data are much more helpful when they gather the data themselves. They can do this by watching video or listening to audio recordings of a lesson, looking at student achievement data, or reviewing data from students' comments about the lesson gathered during interviews, classroom discussions, or exit tickets.

The greatest challenge for teachers, as they explore data about instruction, may be to learn to overcome their defensiveness about what the data reveal or imply. Learning, for example, that your ratio of interaction is skewed toward the negative or that a large percentage of students are not learning what you are teaching can be difficult. We are hardwired to explain away such challenging data. All of us have learned, over time, that a powerful way to get through tough days is to use defense mechanisms to keep us from being hurt by difficult data. When we get disappointing data about a lesson, therefore, we are often inclined to minimize the problem, blame others, or find other ways to explain away the problem.

But if we want to learn from data, we need to approach the process with openness and curiosity. The data are the data, not good or bad. Less than perfect data shouldn't be seen as a complete negative judgment of ourselves. Rather, all data, encouraging and discouraging, can be a starting point for learning that will ultimately benefit us and our students.

Coaches

Although we suggest teachers gather their own data as frequently as possible, coaches, of course, can gather data for teachers whenever it is more convenient for teachers. As always, all of the Data Rules apply here, but ensuring reliability—that the coach and teacher both understand what the data mean—is critical. We suggest coaches and teachers co-construct T-charts filled out with examples and nonexamples of each kind of data. Teachers can learn a lot when coaches share data such as ratio of interaction, but only if the coach and the teacher have a shared understanding of what the data are.

Coaches can also provide teachers with an opportunity to see how their students are experiencing instruction by giving them an opportunity to take a close watch of their students by teaching a teacher's class so that the teacher can take time to observe and think about each student, as is explained in the form below.

CLOSE WATCH OBSERVATIONS

A "close watch" is an opportunity for you to take some time to consider your students from a different, deeper perspective than is usually possible when you are doing the complex, busy work of teaching. That is, the goal of a close watch is to provide an opportunity for you to try to see what lies beneath your students' behaviors, so you can better understand what they are thinking, feeling, and needing.

Here are a few guidelines for how to conduct a close watch, but since this is an open approach to observation, don't feel constricted by these suggestions. The most important objective of this task is to slow down and take the time to look carefully at every student.

GUIDELINES FOR A CLOSE WATCH

1. Find a space to sit where you can best see all students and where you will be able to write notes.

2. Try to empty your mind, so to speak, of all preconceptions you might have about students. Look at your students with curiosity as if you are seeing them for the very first time.

3. Try to jot down a few notes (maybe at least three) about every student. You can do this by taking notes on a seating chart for every student or by simply listing students' names and writing your notes underneath. If your class is too large for you to take notes on all students, consider taking notes on a sample of the class.

4. Look at each student and ask yourself, "What are they feeling? What does the student need?"

5. Ask yourself, "What do I feel about each student? Where does my emotion come from?"

6. Consider drawing a picture of each student to make them really present in your mind. (Don't worry about the quality of the drawings because they are only for you to see.)

7. If you don't want to draw, ask yourself, "If I was drawing a picture, what would I include in my drawing? What makes this student unique? What do I see that tells me something about this student?"

AFTERWARDS

Write some notes about your thoughts about the class. What did you learn? What surprised you? Were there any patterns in what you saw? In light of what you've seen, do you want to do anything different moving forward?

If you work in a school where you can work with a coach, consider discussing your observations with a coach and making plans for next steps.

Administrators

The data described in this chapter are especially helpful for administrators who take a coaching approach to leadership, explicitly separating observation coaching from evaluation. Thus, administrators could suggest teachers consider one or more of the kinds of data described here when they coach teachers around setting goals for improvement—ideally PEERS goals, as described in Chapter 4. Administrators can also gather the data and share them with teachers whenever that might be helpful.

Lastly, administrators can offer to teach a lesson so that teachers can do a close watch of their students. The conversations about students' emotions and needs that occur after the close watch could be a valuable learning opportunity for both teachers and administrators.

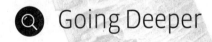 Going Deeper

Many books have described what observers should look for when they watch teachers teach. Perhaps the most widely used guide for observing teachers is Charlotte Danielson's *Enhancing Professional Practice* (2007), which organizes observations around four domains: Domain 1: planning and preparation; Domain 2: learning environments; Domain 3: learning experiences; and Domain 4: principled teaching.

Another frequently used teacher observation model is Robert Marzano and Michael Toth's *Teacher Evaluation That Makes a Difference* (2013), also built around four domains: standards-based planning, standards-based instruction, conditions for learning, and professional responsibilities.

There are many other popular approaches to observing teachers, but regardless of the model you choose, we suggest that it be used in a way that recognizes the importance of the Data Rules described in this book.

PUTTING IT ALL TOGETHER

is about

integrating various kinds of data
to foster better student learning
and well-being

*through
leadership and observation
by the*

*through
the Impact Cycle
guided by the*

*through
self-reflection and learning
done by the*

Principal

Instructional
Coach

Teacher

CHAPTER 8

PUTTING IT ALL TOGETHER

The kinds of data described in this book are powerful on their own, but they can also be gathered in combination. We have included here one example of a data-gathering form that combines many of the forms of data discussed in this book. However, the best combination is likely one that educators custom make for their own unique setting. You can skip this chapter if your team is engaged in transparent communication grounded in objective data when making decisions, but we have a hunch everyone can benefit from reflecting about how we put all of the Data Rules pieces together.

CHAPTER RESOURCES
Access charts, diagrams, research, and resources from this chapter.

The whole is greater than the sum of its parts.

ARISTOTLE

Schools are places of vitality, filled with educators, staff, and students engaged in the process of learning. Yet, too often, we notice educators can feel alone, unintentionally isolated from the larger shared mission to impact student learning. This can happen for a variety of reasons, but in our experience the path toward putting it all together begins in partnership—shared connection—with the other dedicated human beings standing beside you (or at least in the room next to you!). We believe that data can be a bridge between professionals, opening much-needed dialogue, democratizing communication, and providing a clear vision to align everyone's efforts. In the examples below, you can see how members of a school community embrace using data in different ways, all in service of the greater desire to improve outcomes for students, and in the process become better together.

The 20-minute high-impact survey combines student data (e.g., time on task and disruptions) with teaching data (e.g., ratio of interactions and instructional time). Different schools will create different forms. What matters is that schools identify the data that will have the greatest positive impact on teaching quality and, as a result, the greatest positive impact on student learning and well-being.

How to Put Together All the Data

To provide a picture of how different kinds of data may be used in ways that are consistent with the Data Rules, we've created a fictional school named Pleasant Grove Middle School in a town somewhere in the middle of the United States. Let's consider how the

20-MINUTE HIGH-IMPACT SURVEY

Community Building

Time on Task

MINUTES	STUDENTS	ON TASK	% ON TASK
:10			
:20			

Ratio of Interactions

REINFORCING	CORRECTING

Disruptions

Teacher / Student Talk

Instructional Time

Check which of the following teaching practices were present and record the number of minutes for each:

CHECK	PRACTICE/ACTIVITY	MINUTES	CHECK	PRACTICE/ACTIVITY	MINUTES
	Beginning routine			Transition time	
	Stories			Quizzes	
	Thinking prompts				
	Cooperative learning				
	Experiential learning				
	Labs				
	Seat work				
	Direct instruction				

Kinds of Questions

OPEN	CLOSED

Levels of Questions

KNOWLEDGE	SKILL	BIG IDEA

Planning, Assessment, Learning

	YES	NO
Teacher clearly states learning target for the lesson		
Teacher clearly describes success criteria for the student learning		
Teacher gathers data showing whether or not students are learning		
Teacher modifies teaching or learning to improve student achievement based on data gathered		

principal, coach, and many of the teachers at Pleasant Grove might use the ideas in this book to fuel growth in student learning and well-being.

Principal

Dr. Kanesha Williams, the principal at Pleasant Grove, was responsible for bringing *Data Rules* to her school. Kanesha is a runner, and she learned how powerful data can be when she worked to improve her running. "Knowing how fast I was running, my heart rate, how many kilojoules my watch said I was burning, even knowing how much I weighed, all helped me get better—all that data helped me run a personal best in the half-marathon," she said. "If data could help me improve as a runner, I was sure that data could help us improve as a school," she added.

After a *Data Rules* workshop, Kanesha was committed to "walking the talk" by deepening her understanding of all of the kinds of data that were described. She visited a lot of classrooms, gathered data, and then reflected on what had and had not worked until she was confident that she could describe and gather data effectively. She also took to heart the 10 Data Rules (described in Chapter 2) and tried to apply them in all of her evaluation and coaching conversations with teachers.

Kanesha's deep understanding of data helped her see more when she visited teachers' classrooms. For example, she liked to do learning walks through her school (she preferred the term "learning walks" to the more commonly used "walkthroughs") to better understand what was happening at Pleasant Grove. *Data Rules* gave her a set of guidelines to organize her observations. When it comes to really seeing what is happening, as Alexandra Horowitz explains in *On Looking* (2013), "Everyone needs a mechanism to select what, out of all the things in the world, they should both look for and at, and what they should ignore" (p. 108). Kanesha saw learning walks as a simple, informal way for her to better understand what was happening in her school. *Data Rules* gave her "mechanisms" that focused her observations and helped her see more.

When Kanesha evaluated teachers, she applied the Data Rules as best she could so that her evaluations were more beneficial for students and teachers. She also advocated within her district for an evaluation system that was focused on objective data, and she proposed modifications to the evaluation system so that her evaluations dealt with most of the kinds of data included in *Data Rules* because they were focused on impacting student learning. Eventually, the district evaluation form looked a lot like the 20-minute survey included above.

Prior to an evaluation observation, Kanesha met with teachers individually to explain that the evaluation was not a one-and-done activity at Pleasant Grove, and that she would be talking with teachers about data all the time as they tried their best to meet the needs of all their students. She emphasized that the kinds of data people gather help them see things that they might not see without the data.

During the pre-observation meetings, Kanesha went through all of the items on the evaluation form and ensured that both she and the teacher she was going to observe had a mutually agreed-upon understanding of the kinds of data to be gathered. She wanted teachers to know that evaluation was not a "gotcha" activity but rather a learning activity for both the teachers and her.

Kanesha also offered to video record the lesson and share it with teachers so that they could watch and evaluate their lesson prior to their evaluation conversation. Not every teacher wanted to watch video of their lessons, but most did, and when teachers did watch recordings of their lessons with the evaluation form in hand, they had conversations that were more equal, meaningful, and productive.

One way that Kanesha supported her teachers was by making it possible for them to do a close watch of their students. That is, she offered to teach a lesson and told the teachers, "You don't need to worry about what I do in your classroom. Watch your students. What are they doing? What do they need? Are they answering questions? How do you feel about the students' engagement? Where do those feelings come from in the data you are collecting? Jot notes down about every student, and then we can talk about what you see."

One Data Rule that Kanesha especially took to heart was the rule that data should foster hope. She had learned that hope involves three components: (a) a goal, some-thing to hope for; (b) pathways to the goal; and (c) agency, a belief that we can follow that pathway to the goal (Lopez, 2013). To ensure that data fostered hope, Kanesha partnered with teachers to set goals based on what data revealed and then asked coaching questions to invite the teachers to identify strategies (pathways) they might implement to hit the goal. Then she and the teachers collaboratively identified what data they would gather to show that they were moving closer to the goal (thus building agency). When teachers were unsure of what data to collect, Kanesha was able to share options from *Data Rules* for teachers to select.

Another major way in which Kanesha fostered hope was by suggesting that teachers partner with their building instructional coach, Sarah Boulez. The teachers who worked with Sarah moved through an entire Impact Cycle, a coaching cycle we've designed specifically to build and foster hope in teachers and students (Knight, 2018; see also Chapter 4).

Instructional Coach

Sarah Boulez has been an instructional coach for eight years. To support her in her role, Kanesha made sure that Sarah had extensive professional development (PD) related to instructional coaching, and she participated in the Instructional Coaching Group's (ICG) online virtual institute. Sarah has particularly worked on her communication and leadership skills, and through the coaching she has received from her district coaching champion, the PD she has experienced, the collaborative learning she's experienced with other district coaches, and watching her own coaching on video and reflecting on her practice, she has learned to ask more and talk less, approaching each coaching interaction with curiosity and openness.

Sarah uses *The Impact Cycle* (Knight, 2018) to structure her coaching cycles, and she and her colleagues have created an instructional playbook (Knight, 2021) that she refers to almost daily. The playbook contains the highest-leverage teaching strategies that she and her colleagues use to help teachers hit their goals. Sarah and her fellow coaches in the district continually update the playbook as they learn more about what strategies are most helpful for teachers and students and as they learn better ways to implement the identified strategies. The playbook is a living document, continually being improved by the research and practice of the district's instructional coaches.

Sarah and her colleagues have also acquired a deep understanding of *Data Rules*. They participated in the workshop that Kanesha organized for coaches and administrators, and they deepened their knowledge by observing classes and comparing notes with their fellow coach colleagues to ensure that their observations are reliable. In her years at Pleasant Grove, Sarah has used *Data Rules* with dozens of teachers in a partnership approach separate from Kanesha's formal evaluations. By separating observation from evaluation, Kanesha's leadership sets a growth mindset tone, fostering educator efforts to try out new practices for their own professional reflection and Sarah's feedback without fear and as a healthy part of improving their practice prior to any formal evaluation.

One of the first teachers Sarah partnered with was Charlotte Abbado. Charlotte had been teaching at Pleasant Grove for many years, and although she had been asked to become an administrator on many occasions, she had always turned down the invitation because, she said, "the kids are why I get up every day, and I can't imagine not teaching." Charlotte was highly respected by teachers and administrators alike at Pleasant Grove and had taught many of her fellow teachers' children.

Sarah approached Charlotte first because she knew other teachers would likely want to be coached if Charlotte was coached, because everyone held Charlotte in such high regard. This turned out to be exactly what happened, as teachers began to realize that Sarah could make their lives easier and help them reach more students.

Charlotte set and reached many goals when partnering with Sarah. At first, they worked on achievement goals, which led to Charlotte beginning to use more forma-tive assessment in her class. Then they partnered to implement the components of the science of reading, which was a district initiative. This year, they ultimately focused on the emotional engagement goal of psychological safety.

Charlotte and Sarah did two things to get a clear picture of reality before Charlotte set the goal. First, Sarah video recorded one of Charlotte's lessons. When Charlotte watched video of her students, she started to have concerns about their willingness to speak in class. Charlotte then asked Sarah to interview some of the students so that they could both get a better understanding of students' emotional engagement. Data from the interviews confirmed what the video and observation suggested: Students didn't feel safe speaking in class. As a result, Charlotte decided her coaching goal would be related to psychological safety.

Getting clear on something as mercurial and imprecise as psychological safety wasn't easy. Teacher and coach both realized that no goal would be perfect. They decided to measure psychological safety by giving students an exit ticket at the end of each week, asking students two questions: "On a scale of 1–5[1], how safe have you felt in class this week?" and "What could be done to help you feel safer?" Charlotte set the goal that 90% of students would report that they were a 4 or 5 on the scale. "Of course, I want every student to feel safe," she said, "but I will feel we've done something important if a large majority of the students feel safe."

At first, Charlotte and Sarah were a little shocked by the students' responses. Many students reported not feeling safe and circled 1 and 2 on the scale. Students wrote about their lack of trust in the school and their teacher. They also wrote about many things outside the classroom, including relationship issues and online bullying, that eroded their feelings of safety.

Based on these data, Charlotte decided that the first strategy she'd try would be to increase her positive interactions with students, so Sarah started to gather ratio-of-interaction data. The results improved, and the classroom felt like a more positive place, but many students still reported that they were a long way from feeling safe.

After talking with Sarah, Charlotte enthusiastically agreed to the idea of conducting an interaction analysis (IA), so she started to gather IA data (see Chapter 7). What emerged quickly was that, as Charlotte said, "I don't know what to talk about with the students." So, they surveyed the students about their interests, and Charlotte subsequently started talking with students about the topics they identified. She even pushed herself to learn more about the music, sports, games, and books her students loved. In the beginning, these conversations sometimes felt a bit awkward because Charlotte didn't know a lot about Minecraft, Pokémon, or Kendrick Lamar, but she persevered, and most of her students appreciated their teacher taking the time to talk about what they loved.

---

[1]There is no consensus on the best range for a Likert scale (1–4, 5, 6, 7, 10). A 1–5 scale, however, has the advantage of being easy to sort, perhaps grouping results into three categories: 4–5, 3, 1–2); also, it is easy for teachers to set a goal, for example, that 90% of the responses are in the 4–5 range.

The students eventually hit the goal, but Charlotte still wasn't totally satisfied. Certainly, her classroom was different. More students were speaking up and sharing ideas. She felt she had a real connection with almost all of her students, but she wondered if they had changed their ratings on the exit tickets just because they liked her more. "Whether or not the data are influenced by my relationship with students," Charlotte said, "my class is reporting feeling safer, and my students are talking and learning, and I know my kids better. I consider that to be a big win, but I want to keep working to better understand and respond to my students."

Sarah was also partnering with Soon-Chan Park, a language arts teacher in 7th grade. Soon-Chan was a published poet, and he was passionate about the power of words. He had a poster of Hamza Yusuf prominently displayed in his classroom with Yusuf's quotation, "Don't ever diminish the power of words. Words move hearts and hearts move limbs."

Soon-Chan came to Sarah because his students' writing, he said, was hard to read. "They write the way they talk, in long ungrammatical statements. They have voices, and they have things they want to say, but too often I can't understand what it is they're saying. If they're going to succeed or make a difference in life, people need to be able to understand what they are writing. I want them to learn how to write sentences."

Sarah felt an obligation to mention different ways of getting a clear picture of reality such as those she had used with Charlotte, but Soon-Chan didn't think that was necessary, claiming, "I know what my students can't do and what I want them to do. I want them to write complete sentences." Sarah had taught mathematics, so she didn't have a deep knowledge of grammar, but Soon-Chan was quickly able to describe his goal to her as they journeyed through the Impact Cycle together. "I want the students' sentences to be grammatically correct, and I want at least one-third of the sentences to involve complicated sentence structures such as compound or complex sentences. That," Soon-Chan said, "would be awesome."

Sarah suggested that they write a single-point rubric for correct sentences. "Why don't you tell me the characteristics of a complete sentence, and I'll be your secretary," Sarah said. Soon-Chan explained that a good sentence "should have a subject and a verb, a capital letter, and end punctuation. Each clause in a good sentence should contain one complete thought that can stand on its own. That's probably the most important characteristic. That sentences are made up of complete thoughts, not just a stream of disorganized ideas and feelings."

Together, Sarah and Soon-Chan then created a single-point rubric for complete sentences, and Soon-Chan set the goal that 100% of his students would get 5 out of 5 three times in a row on the rubric. Soon-Chan planned to grade student assignments using the rubric, but he soon learned that it took way too much time for him to frequently grade paragraphs written by all 150 students.

After talking with Sarah, Soon-Chan decided on two strategies: (a) to teach the students how to use the rubric to review their own writing and do a peer review and (b) to use checks for understanding daily to ensure that students understood what he was teaching. Soon-Chan also realized that, although his 100% goal was ambitious and noble, not all students would be able to hit that goal every day. As a result, he modified his goal to state that 90% of students would get 5 out of 5 on the rubric independently and that the remaining students would be able to get 5 out of 5 with support.

Soon-Chan and Charlotte were only two of the teachers Sarah worked with that year. However, in each case data stood at the heart of her instructional coaching. Data helped Sarah and the collaborating teachers set goals, and data gathered each week helped teachers see what worked and what didn't work. The results from frequent data checks helped teachers and coaches identify adaptations that needed to be made so that instruction helped students succeed. Data also helped motivate students and teachers because, as students made progress toward the goal, everyone was more hopeful and more confident that the goal would be met.

Teachers

As the only coach in a school with more than 50 teachers, Sarah wasn't able to work with all the teachers at the same time, so many teachers, sometimes after brief conversations with colleagues, Sarah, or Kanesha, used data on their own to guide their inquiry into the learning happening in their classrooms.

Several teachers were very interested in assessing students' emotional engagement. At the end or beginning of each week, they gave students exit tickets asking them questions related to emotional engagement. For example, one teacher asked students, "On a scale of 1–10, how positive has this week been for you?" and "What could your teacher do to help you have more positive experiences?" Another teacher asked, "How safe did you feel in our classroom this week?" and "What could I do to help you feel safer?"

Kanesha provided ongoing encouragement to the teachers who were gathering data on emotional engagement, and at least twice a year, she held schoolwide conversations about students' emotional engagement at Pleasant Grove. She asked teachers to give each student an exit ticket at the end of the first period with an emotional engagement question such as "Do you feel safe in school?" or "What do you want your teachers to know about you that they don't know?" Then she asked teachers to review the exit tickets, look for patterns, and come to a staff meeting prepared to discuss what the exit ticket data revealed.

These conversations were always powerful. Students' comments clearly revealed that students were dealing with serious challenges. The meetings prompted some beautiful expressions of compassion from educators, and everyone felt much more aware of how students were doing. Also, perhaps even more important, the meetings led staff to identify strategies they could use to increase emotional engagement, such as learning more about students' interests, meeting students at the classroom door at the start of the day, scheduling more one-to-one conversations with students, and using interaction analysis to increase student engagement.

Over the years, teachers looked at other aspects of engagement, often through the use of video. Many teachers set their smartphones up at the front of their class, turned the cameras toward their students, and then later watched videos of lessons to see how the type and level of questions they asked affected the number and the quality of student responses. Other teachers watched video recordings of their lessons to see how their teaching affected the number of disruptions in class. Some teachers used experience sampling (see Chapter 5) to see how cognitively engaged students were during various learning activities.

Most teachers, in one way or another, gathered data to formatively assess student learning. For example, Jordan Bernstein, a 6th grade science teacher, gave his students an exit ticket each class with a question about the content they had been taught that day. Then, in between classes, Jordan grouped students' answers, wrapped each group in an elastic band, and attached a sticky note with the number of tickets in each group. The next day, Jordan then retaught content based on how students had answered the question on the exit ticket the previous day. In that way, data from the exit tickets were the point of departure for classroom learning every day.

Ellie Gardiner was an 8th grade language arts teacher who believed that students needed to develop their capacity to appreciate literature. "Literature," she'd say, "can deepen anyone's experience of the world, but people have to know how to read it." For Ellie, that meant, in part, that readers understood and could apply some key literary terms. "It's not just that they can regurgitate a bunch of definitions and terms," she said, "readers need to understand how to apply those terms or concepts so each work is opened up to them as they read."

Like Jordan, Ellie gave students an exit ticket every day that asked students to explain and identify how a key literary term was used in whatever work they had read that day. For example, she might ask, "What is a metaphor and what is an example of a metaphor used in today's poem?" Ellie had a list of the 20 key terms she wanted students to learn, and each day she reviewed the exit tickets and noted what percentage of students correctly identified the term. "If they meet me at Target 15 years from now," she said, "I want them to tell me I taught them how to read and love literature."

Ellie also asked students to write suggestions on the exit tickets for what she could do to help them learn. The data showed two things: (a) students weren't all learning the terms, and (b) many wanted more practice time applying the terms. So, Ellie video recorded three lessons to assess instructional time, and she found some simple adjustments she could make so that there was more time for practice. Ultimately, the data she got from exit tickets and video helped Ellie make changes that empowered her students to open up and enjoy what they read.

At Pleasant Grove, data helped teachers like Jordan, Ellie, and Charlotte understand how well all students were learning and helped students see how well they were learning. Data were a part of the teachers' overall instructional plan. Teachers clarified the outcomes for student learning, identified success criteria, integrated engaging learning activities, and then provided helpful feedback. Data were the GPS for each learning experience. Data revealed whether learning was on track or whether teachers needed to recalculate. Ultimately, data revealed when students and teachers together arrived at the intended destinations for learning.

Conclusion

When data are used by the principal, coach, and teachers at Pleasant Grove, it helps teachers identify student goals and monitor progress toward those goals. In a very real sense, data foster hope. Data cut through the mists and help educators see what students need and see what isn't working. For this reason, data need to be at the heart of any improvement effort because data help teachers get better. And when teachers get better, so do students.

 To Sum Up

This chapter described various ways in which educators can integrate the kinds of data described:

» Schools can create a comprehensive observation tool similar to the 20-minute survey described in this chapter but tailored to the unique needs and pedagogical approaches used in their settings.

» Principals, like Dr. Kanesha Williams, can advocate for objective data, the option of video, as a part of evaluation. They can also foster hope by helping teachers use data to identify goals and monitor progress, and they can help teachers understand their students better by teaching a lesson while their teachers do a close watch.

» Coaches, like Sarah Boulez, can use data in the context of the Impact Cycle, helping teachers set goals and make instructional plans by video recording teachers' lessons, interviewing students, or helping teachers to create rubrics students give to other students so students can peer-assess each other's writing.

» Teachers, like Jordan Bernstein and Ellie Gardener, can use data within the context of formative assessment so that they and their students know how well they are learning and so that they can adjust their teaching to increase student success—measured by data from formative assessments.

Making It Real

Students

Students have enormous potential to help with professional learning in schools. Who are better qualified than students to comment on how well they are learning, what helps and hinders their learning and engagement, and what can be done to improve their learning experiences? What makes listening to students even more compelling is that when students have a voice in their learning, they are much more engaged.

Teachers

Many of the kinds of data described in this book can easily be used by teachers to see their teaching and see student learning and engagement more clearly. That is, teachers can use video, checks for understanding, close watches, rubrics, and so on to see their classes more clearly. The kinds of data described here can also be integrated into formative assessment so teachers can adjust students' learning experiences to increase student success. Our perspective is that data are most powerful when gathered with a coach who helps teachers set and hit powerful goals targeted to impact student learning.

Coaches

Data stand at the heart of the Impact Cycle. Effective coaches partner with teachers to help them get a clear picture of reality, set goals, monitor progress, and make adjustments based on what the data reveal until goals are met. This is when data are most helpful—when they help teachers see what they might not otherwise see and when they help teachers see the progress they are making. Effective coaches are, in part, data coaches, but ultimately the data are only helpful if they empower teachers to empower students to set and hit learning and engagement goals.

Principals

Principals, as we've seen above, can play a crucial role in developing data literacy in schools by providing learning opportunities for educators to develop a shared vocabulary around data, by ensuring coaches have sufficient professional development and time to coach effectively, and by using data effectively themselves. Principals can also ensure that "data" is not a dirty word but instead a key lever for professional learning and part of the school culture of continuous improvement. Finally, principals can promote the human use of data by documenting the progress being made by the students in their school and ensuring that all students are valued and visible.

 # Going Deeper

In addition to the books suggested in the previous chapters, you can significantly expand your understanding of data by reading the following excellent books. Bruce Wellman and Laura Lipton's *Got Data? Now What?* (2012) offers many useful definitions to deepen anyone's understanding of data in a comprehensive, rich book that is also filled with practical strategies. Most important, perhaps, the authors provide useful suggestions for how to engage in dialogue about data in high-performing groups. Rachel D. Roegman, David Allen, Larry Leverett, Scott T. Thompson, and Thomas C. Hatch's *Equity Visits* (2020) describes, as its title would suggest, a process that leaders can use to invite educators from outside their school to visit and look for systemic inequity in the way students are educated in a host school. Finally, Kathryn Boudett, Elizabeth City, and Richard Murnane's *Data Wise* (2005) provides useful information on an improvement process for analyzing standardized test scores and translating those data into action.

REFERENCES

Ainsworth, L., & Donovan, K. (2019). *Rigorous and relevant curriculum design*. International Center for Leadership.

Amabile, T., & Kramer, S. (2011). *The progress principle: Using small wins to ignite joy, engagement, and creativity at work*. Harvard Business Review Press.

Anderson, L. W. and Krathwohl, D. R., et al (Eds..) (2001) *A Taxonomy for Learning, Teaching, and Assessing: A Revision of Bloom's Taxonomy of Educational Objectives*. Allyn & Bacon. Boston, MA (Pearson Education Group)

Armstrong, P. (2010). *Bloom's taxonomy*. Vanderbilt University Center for Teaching.

Biggs, J., & Collis, K. (1981). *Evaluating the quality of learning: The SOLO taxonomy structure of the observed learning outcome*. Academic Press.

Bill and Melinda Gates Foundation. (n.d.). *Better feedback for better teaching: A practical guide to improving classroom observations*. Measures of Effective Teaching (MET) Project. Retrieved from usprogram.gatesfoundation.org/news-and-insights/articles/measures-of-effective-teaching-project

Block, P. (2013). *Stewardship: Choosing service over self-interest*. Berrett-Kohler Publishers.

Bohm, D., & Nicol, L. (1996). *On dialogue*. Routledge.

Boudett, K.P., City, E.A., & Murmane, R.J. (Eds.). (2005). *Data wise: A step-by-step guide to using assessment results to improve teaching and learning.* Harvard Education Press.

Brookhart, S. M. (2013). *How to create and use rubrics for formative assessment and grading.* Association for Supervision & Curriculum Development.

Buckingham, M., & Goodall, A. (2019). *Nine lies about work: A freethinking leader's guide to the real world.* Harvard Business Review Press.

Clinton, J., Cairns, K., Mclaren, P., & Simpson, S. (2014). *Evaluation of the Victorian Deaf Education Institute Real-Time Captioning Pilot Program, Final Report – August 2014.* The University of Melbourne: Centre for Program Evaluation.

Collins, J., & Porras, J. (1994). *Built to last: successful habits of visionary companies.* Harper Business.

Covey, S., Merrill, A. R., & Merrill, R. R. (2016). *First things first.* Free Press.

Csikszentmihalyi, M. (1990). *Flow: The psychology of optimal experience.* Harper & Row.

Csikszentmihalyi, M. (1994). *The evolving self: A psychology for the third millennium.* HarperCollins Publishers Inc.

Danielson, C. (2007). *Enhancing professional practice: A framework for teaching.* Association for Supervision & Curriculum Development.

Dary, T., Pickeral, T., Shumer, R., & Williams, A. (2016). *Weaving student engagement into the core practices of schools.* National Dropout Prevention Center/Network. https://dropoutprevention.org/wp- content/uploads/2016/09/student-engagement-2016-09.pdf

Doran, G T. (1981). There's a S.M.A.R.T. way to write management's goals and objectives. *Management Review, 70* (11), 25-26.

Dyyik, E.H. (2023, March 13). *Number of pupils in secondary education worldwide 2000-2020*. Statista. https://www.statista.com/staistics/1227098/number-of-pupils-in-secondary-education-worldwide/

Edmondson, A. C. (2019). *The fearless organization: Creating psychological safety in the workplace for learning, innovation, and growth*. Hoboken, New Jersey: John Wiley & Sons, Inc.

Erickson, H.L., Lanning, L.A., & French, R. (2017). *Concept-based curriculum and instruction for the thinking classroom*. Corwin.

Fisher, D., & Frey, N. (2014). *Checking for understanding: formative assessment techniques for your classroom*. Association for Supervision & Curriculum Development.

Fisher, D., Frey, Nancy, N., Quaglia, R.J., Smith, D., & Lande, L.L. (2017). *Engagement by design: Creating learning environments where students thrive*. Corwin.

Francis, E. M. (2021). *Deconstructing depth of knowledge: A method and model for deeper teaching and learning*. Solution Tree Press.

Fredrickson, B. M. (2009). *Positivity: Top-notch research reveals the 3-to-1 ratio that will change your life*. Harmony.

Freire, P. (1970). *Pedagogy of the Oppressed*. Continuum.

Fullan, M. (2001). *Leading in a culture of change*. Jossey-Bass.

Gawande, A. (2009). *The checklist manifesto: How to get things right*. Picador.

Godin, S. (2007). *The dip: A little book that teaches you when to quit (and when to stick)*. Portfolio.

Gottman, J. (2001) *The relationship cure: A 5-step guide to strengthening your marriage, family, and friendships*. Harmony.

Grant Halvorson, H. (2012). *Nine things successful people do differently*. Harvard Business Review Press.

Grant, T. (2003). *Coach yourself: Make real change in your life*. Basic Books.

Hattie, J. (2008). *Visible learning: A synthesis of over 800 meta-analyses relating to achievement*. Routledge.

Heath, C., & Heath, D. (2010). *Switch: How to change things when change is hard*. Crown Business.

Heifitz, R.A., Linsky, M., & Grashow, A. (2009). *The practice of adaptive leadership: Tools and tactics for changing your organization and the world*. Harvard Business Press.

Hektner, J.M., Schmidt, J.A., & Csikszentmihalyi, M. (2006). *Experience sampling method: Measuring the quality of everyday life*. Sage Publications, Inc.

Horowitz, A. (2014). *On looking: A walker's guide to the art of observation*. Scribner.

Instructional Coaching Group. (n.d.) *Research*. Retrieved January 31, 2024, from https://www.instructionalcoaching.com/resources/research

Isaacs, W. (1999). *Dialogue: The art of thinking together*. Currency.

Kegan, R., & Lahey, L. (2001). *The real reason people won't change*. Harvard Business Review.

Kelly, D., & Connor, D. (1979). *Emotional cycle of change*. Pfeiffer.

Keltner, D. (2016). *The power paradox: How we gain and lose influence*. Penguin Books.

Kern, M. L. (2022). PERMAH: A useful model for focusing on well-being in schools. In K.-A. Allen, M. J. Furlong, D. Vella-Brodrick, & S. M. Suldo (Eds.), *Handbook of positive psychology in schools: Supporting process and practice* (3rd ed., pp. 12–24). Routledge.

Kline, N. (2020). *The promise that changes everything: I won't interrupt you.* Penguin Life.

Knight, J. (2013). *High-impact instruction: A framework for great teaching.* Corwin.

Knight, J. (2014). *Focus on teaching: Using video for high impact instruction.* Corwin.

Knight, J. (2015). *Better conversations: Coaching ourselves and each other to be more credible, caring, and connected.* Corwin.

Knight, J. (2019). Students on the margins. Coaching for engagement and achievement. *The Learning Professional, 40* (6).

Knight, J. (2021). *The definitive guide to instructional coaching: Seven factors for success.* Association for Supervision & Curriculum Development.

Knight, J. (host). (2023, October 17). Russ Quaglia. *Coaching conversations with Jim Knight.* [Audio podcast episode.]. https://podcasts.apple.com/ca/podcast/russquaglia/id1649791348?i=1000631594224

Knight, J., & Fullan, M. (2010). *Unmistakable impact: A partnership approach for dramatically improving instruction.* Corwin.

Knight, J., & Gaines, M. (2018). *The impact cycle: What instructional coaches should do to foster powerful improvements in teaching.* Corwin.

Knight, J., Hoffman, A., Harris, M., & Thomas, S. (2020). *The instructional playbook: The missing link for translating research into practice.* Association for Supervision & Curriculum Development.

Ho, A. D., & Kane, T. J. (2013). *The reliability of classroom observations by school personnel.* Harvard Graduate School of Education.

Leahy, S., & William, D. (2015). *Embedded formative assessment: practical techniques for K-12 classrooms.* Solution Tree Press.

Lenz, B. K. (2004). *Teaching content to all: Evidence-based inclusive practices in middle and secondary schools.* Pearson/Allyn and Bacon.

Lenz, B.K., Bulgren, J.A., Schumaker, J.B., Deshler, D.D., & Boudah, D.A. (1994). *The unit routine organizer.* Edge Enterprises.

Lenz, B.K., Marrs, R.W., Schumaker, J.B., & Deshler, D.D. (1993). *The lesson organizer routine.* Edge Enterprises.

Lenz, B.K., Schumaker, J.B., Deshler, D.D., & Bulgren, J.A. (1998). *The course organizer routine.* Edge Enterprises.

Lipton, L., & Wellman, B. (2012). *Got data? Now what? Creating and leading cultures of inquiry.* Solution Tree.

Loehr, J., & Schwartz, T. (2003). *The power of full engagement: Managing energy, not time, is the key to high performance and personal renewal.* Free Press.

Lopez, S. (2014). *Making hope happen: Create the future you want for yourself and others.* Atria.

Lopez, S. J., & Sidhu, P. (2013). *In U.S., newer teachers most likely to be engaged at work: Engagement falls about four percentage points after one year at work.* Gallup.

Love, N. Stiles, K., Mundry, S., diRanna, K. (2008). *The data coach's guide to improving learning for all students: Unleashing the power of collaborative inquiry.* Corwin.

Marzano, R. J., & Toth, M. D. (2013). *Teacher evaluation that makes a difference: A new model for teacher growth and student achievement.* Association for Supervision & Curriculum Development.

McTighe, J., Ferrara, S., & Brookhart, S. (2021). *Assessing student learning by design: principles and practices for teachers and school leaders.* Teachers College Press.

Miller, W R., & Rollnick, S. (2002) *Motivational interviewing: Helping people change and Grow* (2nd ed.). The Guilford Press.

Moran, B., & Lennington, M. (2013). *The twelve week year: Get more done in 12 weeks than others do in 12 months*. Wiley.

Moss, C. M., & Brookhart, S. M. (2012). *Learning targets: Helping students aim for understanding in today's lesson*. Association for Supervision & Curriculum Development.

Murphy, K. (2020). *You're not listening: What you're missing and why it matters*. Celadon Books.

The National Professional Development Center on Autism Spectrum Disorder. (n.d.). *Evidence-based practices*. Retrieved December 12, 2023, https://autismpdc. fpg.unc.edu/evidence-based-practices

Oxford English Dictionary (OED). (n.d.). Online edition. https:www.oed.com

Palmer, P. J. (2004). *A hidden wholeness: The journey toward an undivided life*. Jossey-Bass.

Pressfield, S., & Coyne, S. (2002). *War of art: Break through the blocks and win your inner creative battles*. Black Irish Entertainment LLC.

Prochaska, J.O., Norcros, J., & DiClemente, C. (1994). *Changing for good: A revolutionary six-stage program for overcoming bad habits and moving your life positively forward*. Quill.

Przymus, S., Faggella-Luby, M., & Silva, C. (2022). It's only a matter of meaning: From English learners (ELs) and emergent bilinguals (Ebs) to active bilingual learners/users of English (ABLE). *I-LandD Journal—Identity, Language and Diversity, 4*(2), 30-50.

Reinke, W M., Herman, K C., & Sprick, R. (2011). *Motivational interviewing for effective classroom management*. Guilford Press.

Roegman, R.D., Allen, D., Leverett, L., Thompson, S.T., & Hatch, T.C. (2019). *Equity visits: A new approach to supporting equity-focused school and district leadership.* Corwin.

Rosenberg, M. (2003). *Nonviolent communication: A language of life.* Puddledancer Press.

Rumberger, R. W. (2011). *Dropping out: Why students drop out of high school and what can be done about it.* Harvard University Press.

Safir, S., & Dugan, J. (2021). *Street data: A next-generation model for equity, pedagogy, and school transformation.* Corwin.

Schein, E. (2009). *Helping: How to offer, give, and receive help.* Berrett-Kohler Publishers.

Schlechte, P. C. (2011). *Engaging students: The next level of working on the work.* Jossey-Bass.

Seidman, I. (2022). *Interviewing as qualitative research: A guide for researchers in education and the social sciences.* Teachers College Press.

Seligman, M. E. P. (2012). *Flourish: A visionary new understanding of happiness and well-being.* Atria.

Senge, P. M. (2022). *The fifth discipline: The art and practice of the learning organization.* Random House.

Sherrington, T., & Coviglioli, O. (2020). *Teaching WalkThrus: Visual step-by-step guides to essential teaching techniques.* John Catt Educational.

Skyles, T., Sprick, R., & Knight, J. (2022). *Coaching CHAMPS: Building a system of support for all teachers.* Ancora Publishing.

Snyder, C.R. (2003). *The power of hope: You CAN get here from there.* Free Press.

Sprick, R. (2021). CHAMPS: *A proactive and positive approach to classroom management.* Safe and Civil Schools.

Sprick, R., Garrison, M., & Howard, L.H. (1998). *Champs: A proactive and positive approach to classroom management.* Sopris West.

Sprick, R., Knight, J., Reinke, W., & McKale, T. (2006). *Coaching classroom management strategies and tools for administrators and coaches.* Pacific Northwest Publishing.

Stanier, M. B. (2020). *The Advice Trap: Be humble, stay curious & change the way you lead forever.* Get Abstract AG.

Starr, J. (2016). *The coaching manual: Your step-by-step guide to becoming a great coach.* Pearson Business.

Stern, J., Ferraro, K., Duncan, K., & Aleo, T. (2021). *Learning that transfers: Designing curriculum for a changing world (Corwin Teaching Essentials).* Corwin.

Stevens, D. D., & Levin, A. J. (2004). *Introduction to rubrics: An assessment tool to save grading time, convey effective feedback, and promote student learning.* Routledge.

Stiggins, R. J. (2005). *Student-involved formative assessment.* Pearson Merrill Prentice Hall.

Stoltzfus, T. (2005). *Leadership coaching: The disciplines, skills and heart of a Christian coach.* Coach 22.

Stone, D., & Heen, S. (2015). *Thanks for the Feedback: The science and art of receiving feedback well.* Penguin Books.

United Nations. (n.d.). *Welcome to the United Nations.* Retrieved March 4, 2024, from www.un.org

Van Nieuwerburgh, C. (2017). *An introduction to coaching skills: A practical guide.* Sage Publications Ltd.

Vedantam, S. (2022). *Useful Delusions: The power and paradox of the self-deceiving brain*. W.W. Norton & Company.

Wheatley, M. (2002). *Turning to one another: Simple conversations to restore hope to the future*. Berrett-Kohler Publishers.

Wiggins, G., & McTighe, J. (1998). *Understanding by design*. Association for Supervision & Curriculum Development.

Wiseman, L., & McKeown, G. (2010). *Multipliers: How the best leaders make everyone smarter*. HarperBusiness.

INDEX

The letter f following a page locator denotes a figure.

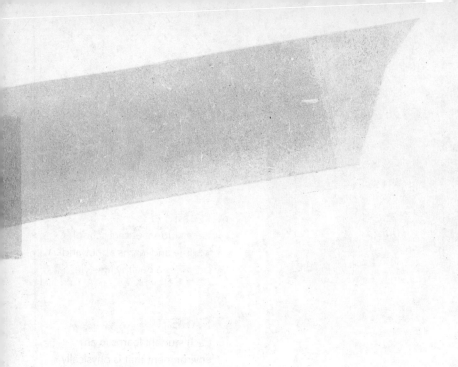

WHOLE CHILD
TENETS

1 **HEALTHY**
Each student enters school healthy and learns about and practices a healthy lifestyle.

2 **SAFE**
Each student learns in an environment that is physically and emotionally safe for students and adults.

3 **ENGAGED**
Each student is actively engaged in learning and is connected to the school and broader community.

4 **SUPPORTED**
Each student has access to personalized learning and is supported by qualified, caring adults.

5 **CHALLENGED**
Each student is challenged academically and prepared for success in college or further study and for employment and participation in a global environment.

**ascd
whole child**

The ASCD Whole Child approach is an effort to transition from a focus on narrowly defined academic achievement to one that promotes the long-term development and success of all children. Through this approach, ASCD supports educators, families, community members, and policymakers as they move from a vision about educating the whole child to sustainable, collaborative actions.

Data Rules relates to the **supported** and **challenged** tenets. *For more about the ASCD Whole Child approach, visit* ***www.ascd.org/wholechild.***